Marketing Your Church

Concepts and Strategies

John J. Considine

Sheed & Ward
Kansas City

Sheed & Ward™ is a service of The National Catholic Reporter Publishing Company.

Library of Congress Cataloguing-in-Publication Data

Considine, John Joseph, 1951-
    Marketing your church : concepts and strategies / John J. Considine.
        p.   cm.
    Includes bibliographical references.
    ISBN: 1-55612-800-2 (pbk. : alk. paper)
    1. Church marketing.   I. Title.
BV652.23.C66   1995
254'.0068'8--dc20   95-14285
                                                         CIP

Published by: Sheed & Ward
                115 E. Armour Blvd.
                P.O. Box 419492
                Kansas City, MO 64141-6492

To order, call: (800) 333-7373

Cover design by John Murello.

Contents

1

Introduction

Marketing — What Is It?

If you were to ask several people to define marketing, you would likely get a variety of definitions. The fact is, marketing is often misunderstood by most people. To some, marketing implies advertising. This is largely a result of the fact that we are surrounded by advertising messages. There is no way an individual can escape the subtle and not so subtle messages of advertising. The typical consumer is said to be exposed to over 2,000 messages daily. Fortunately, we ignore most of them or else our lives would be even more confusing and hectic. In spite of the constant presence of advertising messages and their influence on consumer's purchasing behavior, advertising is actually only one small part of what constitutes marketing.

Similarly, many believe that marketing is basically a sales activity. This misconception is understandable since the result of the marketing process may eventually result in a consumer purchasing a good or service. However, to simply define marketing as merely a purchasing situation is a gross injustice. Again, sales is another small part of the marketing activity.

Having dispensed with these too-common misconceptions of marketing, then what actually is marketing? Again, there are several different ways of defining what is meant by marketing. To begin with, one of the most basic ways of defining marketing is describing it as an "exchange process" — the act of obtaining a desired object from someone by offering something in return. The object may be something tangible (a product) or something intangible (a service) that can be exchanged for money.

Others may interpret marketing as a "matching process" by which an organization provides a marketing mix that most effectively satisfies a consumer's needs or wants. The marketing mix represents an organization's controllable variables, i.e., those variables that the firm can manipulate to most effectively meet the consumer's needs or wants. Marketers generally refer to the marketing mix as being comprised of the 4 P's — product, place, price, and promotion. The belief is that each of these controllable variables is equally important and the combination or mix of these is what will determine the success or failure in appealing to the firm's desired market. The definition also implies the importance of an organization attempting to first identify the needs and wants of those individuals it is trying to attract and then adopting its marketing mix to deliver the desired satisfaction more efficiently and effectively than the competition.

Another perspective comes from the American Marketing Association who in 1985 defined marketing as "The process of planning and executing the conception, pricing, promotion, and distribution of ideas, goods, and services to create exchanges that will satisfy individual and organizational objectives."[1] This implies marketing is a process, not a single activity like advertising or sales, and it incorporates the decisions of an organization relating to the controllable variables as well as the importance of satisfying both the consumer and the organization's goals.

Regardless of which definition of marketing is preferred, the concept of marketing has been increasingly broadened over the last three decades to include not only profit-making organizations, but also the nonprofit sector of society. During the past decade, financial pressures have prompted many nonprofit organizations to pursue more of a marketing orientation. Indeed, many nonprofit organizations have turned to marketing as a means to ensure their survival.

Broadening the Marketing Concept to Churches

Much has been written in recent years concerning the broadening of the marketing discipline to include nonprofit, non-business, and social marketing. Kotler and Levy contended that marketing is a pervasive societal activity that goes considerably beyond the selling of toothpaste, soap, and steel. They further recommend that the marketing concept should be broadened to include the nonprofit sector of society since marketing is a generic activity for all organizations.[2]

Largely as a result of this classic article, practitioners and scholars began turning their attention to the challenge of improving management practice in public agencies and nonprofit institutions. Marketing has become a buzzword of some significance in government agencies, hospitals, universities, transit systems, arts organizations, and social groups.[3]

Some non-business managers are extremely comfortable with the basic philosophy of marketing since it embodies much of their existing approach to management. Many managers of such organizations discovered they had been marketing-oriented without being conscious of it. Such managers do not need to be convinced of the appropriateness of marketing as a management function of their organization.

Over the last 20 years, many different nonprofit organizations have successfully implemented marketing as a critical part of their organizational environment. Similarly, there has been a significant increase in research addressing the utilization of marketing principles in a nonprofit setting. However, there still exists one nonprofit organization that has been extremely slow in accepting the broadened marketing concept — churches.

Challenges Facing Churches

While most churches have been very reluctant in utilizing marketing techniques and very slow in becoming more marketing oriented, the challenges and problems confronting churches today necessitate a more realistic and pragmatic consideration of how a marketing orientation may enable them to best meet the needs of their desired constituents and ultimately grow and prosper.

Churches in America are facing a crisis. The percentage of persons not connected to a church or synagogue in virtually every county of the United States is greater than ever before in the history of the country. For the first time in history, there are more non-Christians than Christians in America. In addition, mainline Protestants, the traditional denominations such as Methodist, Presbyterian, Episcopalian, and the United Church of Christ, have lost more than a quarter of their adherents in the past two decades (see Figure 1.1).[4]

Based on his research on church growth, George Barna found several facts further illuminating the turmoil many churches find themselves in. For instance, he determined that there has been "no growth" in the proportion of the adult population that can be classified as "born again" Christians. (These are people who have made a personal commitment to Jesus Christ, accepting Him as their Lord and Savior). Secondly, he found that since 1970, there has been no appreciable change in the proportion of adults who attend church services at any time during the week. Similarly, attitudinal studies have shown that people's confidence in the church as an institution is declining. Furthermore, only a minority of adults in this nation consider the Christian church to be "relevant for today." Another dramatic finding was that the average Protestant congregation in this country has 50 to 60 adults who regularly attend Sunday morning worship services. Unfortunately, that is often not enough people for a church to prosper — emotionally, financially, or in many cases spiritually. Finally, Barna discovered that community studies conducted in various parts of the country have revealed that a growing number of adults are unfamiliar with the churches in their community. These adults do not even know the names of denominations of the churches in their communities, much less what they teach or otherwise offer.[5]

	1965	1970	1975	1980	1985	1987	1988
American Lutheran Church	2.54	2.54	2.42	2.35	2.33	*	*
Lutheran Church in America	3.14	3.11	2.99	2.92	2.90	*	*
Evang. Luth. Church America					*	5.29	5.25
Lutheran Church-Mo. Synod	2.69	2.79	2.76	2.63	2.63	2.61	2.60
Christian Church (Disciples)	1.92	1.42	1.30	1.18	1.12	1.09	1.07
Episcopal Church	3.43	3.29	2.86	2.79	2.74	2.46	2.45
Presbyterian Church (USA)	3.98	4.04	3.54	3.36	3.05	2.97	2.93
United Church of Christ	2.07	1.96	1.82	1.74	1.68	1.66	1.64
United Methodist Church	11.10	10.50	9.86	9.52	9.19	9.12	9.05

*The Evangelical Lutheran Church in America was organized in 1987, merging the American Lutheran Church, the Lutheran Church in America, and the Association of Evangelical Lutheran Churches.

SOURCE: Yearbook of American & Canadian Churches, 1989, 1990.

Declining Membership in Mainline Denominations (In Millions)
Figure 1.1

Shawchuck, Kotler, Wrenn and Rath have identified other contemporary challenges facing churches. For instance, they contend that secularization of American society points to nonreligious values and institutions (wealth, power, independence, etc.) in displacing religious values and institutions as the motivating factors of persons' attitudes, values, and behavior. Another challenge for congregations is changing demographics manifested in the decline of family life: escalating divorce rates, more children in single-parent homes, broken homes. People are finding themselves increasingly fragmented and disassociated from others.

Perhaps more threatening to churches is the intense competition they face from many sectors: secular activities (movies, sports, travel), religious activities (local congregations, TV ministries, Eastern religions), and human potential offerings (humanism, New Age movement, etc.). While many religious leaders perceive their main competition to be other churches (i.e. mainline church vs evangelical vs independent), Shawchuck, et al contend that with an ever-increasing percentage of Americans claiming no religious affiliation, the prospect pool is large enough to fill every church in town. The more substantial competition are the habits that millions of Americans have developed for their Sunday morning routine. The authors state that in Chicago, the Chicago Bears and Lake Michigan are greater competition to the United Methodist congregations than are the Presbyterians a couple of blocks down the street.[6]

Other factors confronting churches today include attitudinal and behavioral changes on the part of the baby-boom generation. Many young people are not inheriting the religion of their parents but are delaying commitment to a church or synagogue until some nodal event (e.g., the birth of a child), precipitates religious "shopping" behavior. The individual or couple then "sample" congregations until finding one that fits the preferred lifestyle. Increasingly, loyalty to a particular denomination fails to accompany a family when it changes its residence. In addition, research indicates many people no longer believe church or synagogue attendance is essential to their faith. George Gallup, Jr., and Sarah Jones revealed that nationally 76% of American adults felt a person could be a good Christian or Jew without attending a church or synagogue.[7]

All these factors point out that the church is having a difficult time making inroads into the lives and hearts of people. The sad fact is that churches seem to be growing more irrelevant over time to the majority of Americans. Most of the 300,000 churches in

America are not satisfying their congregations and more people are becoming "unchurched" citizens. Many churches appear to have lost touch with their constituents. The severity of these problems call for new approaches to enable churches to make themselves more appealing, relevant, and sensitive to their constituents without compromising their mission. Marketing is such an approach that can assist these congregations, large and small, to accomplish that goal. Marketing can be a vital "tool" to help churches better serve their congregations and society and continue to grow and prosper.

Factors Inhibiting Church Marketing

While marketing can be a vital tool in helping churches effectively satisfy the spiritual needs and wants of their constituents, there are several factors currently hindering churches from becoming more marketing-oriented. These factors help explain why so many churches are only beginning to examine marketing and why the term "church marketing" is so new.

To begin with, many church leaders are very skeptical as to the use of marketing in church settings. To many, marketing does not suggest a biblical practice. To the skeptics, it may be logical to use marketing techniques to sell toothpaste or cars, but it appears almost immoral to use the same concepts in a religious framework. As stated previously, many misinterpret marketing to be synonymous with either advertising or sales — neither of which generally suggests biblical ideals.

Similarly, there has been a great deal of antagonism and mistrust towards a marketing orientation exemplified by many church leaders, in spite of the fact that implementing marketing concepts and techniques might enhance their church's growth and survival. Admittedly, most churches are not exactly known for setting trends or embracing change. Although marketing has been an accepted discipline in many profit and nonprofit organizations, many church leaders consider even speaking of marketing a church as "the next best thing to blasphemy." When George Barna wrote *Marketing the Church* in 1988, he was overwhelmed by the reactions of many church leaders. Many pastors wrote him off as a heretic, a young, aggressive, worldly fellow. In addition, some Christian bookstores "banned" the book, refusing to expose their austereness to a volume filled with such scandalous thought.[8]

The misconceptions of marketing and resulting antagonism shared by many church leaders can be partially explained by the fact that the training most church leaders receive generally concerns only religious matter. For a local church to be a successful business, it must impact a growing share of its market area.

Unfortunately, the pastor will be judged on how smoothly and efficiently the church is run — i.e., based on the businesslike performance of the church — an area where he/she has received no training. Without any knowledge or training in marketing, the typical pastor, undoubtedly, may be hesitant to turn to this orientation to help keep the church solvent and make it appealing enough for people to attend.

Another common conception of marketing activities is that it is too expensive or a waste of money. The belief is not uncommon among many nonprofit leaders since they are constantly faced with making decisions with scarce resources at their disposal.

A few years ago, I was doing some consulting for a mass transit agency at which the director had a very negative attitude towards marketing. This director had spent a large portion of their allocated marketing budget on local television advertising spots. The advertisements, while informative and somewhat creative, did not result in any significant increase in ridership. From his perspective, marketing was synonymous with advertising and the net effect was a waste of money.

Unfortunately, many church leaders may share the same opinion as this transit director. At some point, they may have spent some of their scarce resources on advertising, direct mail, sponsored events, etc., and not seen any appreciable increase in attendance or other benefits to the church. Obviously, church leaders, while operating with limited resources, must be extremely careful in allocating their funds. They must be careful to choose effective, low-cost approaches and always be concerned about the return or impact of their marketing expenditures.

Benefits of Church Marketing

While marketing is not intended to be a panacea for churches, those churches who become more marketing-oriented may experience certain benefits that will aid its growth and survival.

To begin, a marketing-oriented church will have a sharper vision as to the spiritual needs of its constituents, and be able to more efficiently try to provide the types of worship or programs that satisfy these needs. In general, the marketing concept implies that the organization attempts to identify and satisfy the needs and wants of the specific group it is trying to attract. For a church, this infers that they first try to identify and understand the specific needs of its constituents and/or the specific segment of the population it is trying to attract (Chapter 4 on Marketing Research for Churches will provide the details on this step.) Secondly, once having determined these specific needs, the church can then effectively plan what types of offerings or services will fulfill these needs. (Chapter 5 on Developing a Marketing Plan for Churches will address these issues.)

Similarly, a marketing-oriented church that incorporates such proven marketing techniques as market research and strategic planning will be able to more efficiently allocate its limited resources and ideally receive more impact for its expenditures. A church can no longer afford to be all things to all people. In addition, many churches are facing severe financial difficulties due to dwindling membership, the recession, lack of consumer confidence, etc. Like any other business, a church must be extremely careful in determining when to spend these limited resources and how to maximize the effect of their spending.

Since one of the goals of many churches is to "spread the word" and bring new members into a relationship with God, a marketing orientation will enable these churches to clearly identify what types of people they are trying to attract and how best to try and influence their behavior to first come to church. Again, a mass marketing approach is no longer feasible. In the future, churches must clearly segment the market like other for-profit and nonprofit organizations have pursued. (Chapter 3 on Market Segmentation will discuss separation strategies for churches.)

Finally, a marketing-oriented church will be able to be more in touch with its environment and to specific problems, issues or opportunities within the community it serves. A marketing orientation implies being aware of what is going on in the local community. Again, this awareness implies actions to help influence some community residents to attend church and then begin their "walk with God." Furthermore, by being included in the community and demonstrating God's love for others, a church can gain respect and admiration from those in the community and be a recognizable, positive influence in local affairs. Such involvement in local issues can also energize church members, or they can actively demonstrate Christian life and see how their specific actions of love and mercy can touch others.

Plan of this Book

As a Christian and a marketing professor, I believe very strongly in the use of marketing techniques to help a church grow, not only in attracting new members, but also in reaching out to the community and benefiting society. My intent in writing this book is to argue for church marketing, pointing out how certain marketing techniques which have worked well for profit and nonprofit organizations can also enable churches to identify and accomplish specific goals. Through the book I will point out definite benefits in utilizing marketing techniques and describe the use of these techniques as appropriate for churches. Being well aware of most churches' limited resources, not only financial but also including time and staff, I will consistently offer special strategies or tips specifically for churches. Similarly, I will discuss the problems or limitations of the techniques that are discussed. My hope is to offer a readable, practical, and logical case to convince church leaders to be more receptive to the concept of marketing and inform them of the benefits it may provide them and their constituents.

The specific outline of the book is as follows. The next chapter describes what I believe a market-driven church implies. Specifically, I will discuss the 4 P's of a marketing mix from a church perspective. In addition, I will discuss the challenges churches face in their macro-environment — what I call the uncontrollable forces. The next three chapters constitute the basics of obtaining information and developing appropriate goals and objectives for churches. Included in these chapters will be topics such as market segmentation strategies for churches, market research, and strategic planning. These topics are discussed in a manner that is relevant for churches, and appropriate strategies for church implementation will be offered. The next section includes chapters specifically related to the 4 P's of church marketing. Chapter 6 will address tactics and strategies involving product, place, and price decisions and their implications. Chapter 7 will offer appropriate promotional strategies for churches to more effectively communicate with their intended publics. The next section will contain a few special church marketing topics, especially appropriate for the 90s. First, I will examine the technique of direct mail, one of the fastest growing segments of direct marketing, and how it can be utilized by churches. Second, I will examine the largest potential target for churches who wish to grow — baby boomers, roughly 76 million Americans from between 1946 and 1964, many of whom remain unchurched. This generation, unparalleled in modern times, possesses certain unique characteristics and behaviors which church leaders must understand if they are going to be successful in appealing to their spiritual needs.

Endnotes

1. Louis E. Boone and David L. Kurtz, (1992) *Contemporary Marketing,* Fort Worth, TX: The Dryden Press, p. 6.

2. Philip Kotler and Sidney J. Levy (1969), "Broadening the Marketing Concept," *Journal of Marketing,* January 1969, p. 10.

3. Christopher H. Lovelock and Charles B. Weinberg, (1989), *Public and Nonprofit Marketing,* Redwood City, California: The Scientific Press.

4. Thomas A. Stewart, (1989), "Turning Around the Lord's Business," *Fortune,* 9/25/89, p. 116.

5. George Barna, (1988), *Marketing the Church,* Colorado Springs, Colorado: Navpress, pp. 21-22.

6. Norman Shawchuck, Philip Kotler, Bruce Wrenn and Gustave Roth, (1992), *Marketing For Congregations,* Nashville, TN: Abingdon Press, p. 28.

7. George Gallup, Jr. and Sarah Jones, (1989), *One Hundred Questions and Answers in America,* Princeton, NJ: The Princeton Religious Research Center.

8. George Barna, *Church Marketing,* Ventura CA: Regal Books, 1992, p. 13.

2

Defining a
Marketing-Oriented Church

What Is Meant by a Marketing Orientation?

Although many firms, both profit and nonprofit, are clearly marketing-oriented in their pursuit of satisfying both their target market's needs and wants and their organizational goals and objectives, this concept is the result of a slow evolution over the last 80 or 90 years. Back in the early 1900s, the marketing concept was unheard of and most firms could be described as being production-oriented. As the name implies, the emphasis was on producing as much as possible as efficiently as possible. The early decades of this century were accompanied by the introduction of many labor and time-saving production techniques. At the time, the emphasis on production and not the consumer was very appropriate. For most commodities, there was a great imbalance between supply and demand, since the demand for the commodity far exceeded the available supply. Likewise, the initial production costs of the commodities being produced were often quite high, which put it out of reach of most consumers. These two conditions pressured firms to look for ways to improve production, to correct the demand-supply imbalance, and also to bring down the costs of these commodities.

Henry Ford was certainly one of the pioneers of the production orientation. Ford's vision was to make a car affordable to the masses. With his vision, he incorporated numerous production innovations and assembly line improvements that resulted in production of the Model T Ford that was affordable to middle-class Americans.

While his expertise was on production, Ford cared little about understanding the needs and wants of the American consumer. His total disregard for the consumer can be summed up by one of his famous quotes: "You can have any color car you want as long as it's black." Basically, Ford was saying to the consumer, "Here is our product offering; it's affordable and available; take it or leave it."

Over the next several decades, the supply-demand imbalance was stabilized for many commodities and the initial high costs of many commodities came down as a result of many production-related improvements and the learning curve. As a result, many firms found that being solely concerned with production was not practical since consumers had more and more choices to choose from. Many firms began to increase their emphasis towards a sales orientation in order to find consumers for their product and convince them to buy it. The basic notion of what marketers refer to as a "sales orientation" is that customers will resist buying goods and services that are not essential, or necessities, and the firm must utilize various promotional techniques, such as advertising, personal selling, or sales promotion to influence them to buy.

Again, this orientation, now focusing on sales rather than production, also neglected to identify consumers' needs and wants. Firms produced products and services they deemed important or essential and then tried to influence and persuade consumers to buy them. After World War II, firms returned to turning out consumer goods in record numbers, and found that this created a need for more of a consumer orientation.

In essence, firms realized that with all the competition and, as well, a strong buyer's market, they could no longer neglect what the actual needs and wants of the consumers were. The emphasis had switched from focusing on the seller's needs to focusing on the buyer's needs. This focus on identifying the buyer's needs is what many now referred to as the "marketing concept" or "marketing orientation." Basically, the marketing orientation is a contemporary philosophy inferring that the firm identify the needs and wants of the group it hopes to attract and then adapt itself to delivering the desired satisfaction more efficiently and effectively than the competition.

The definition of a marketing orientation implies a two-step process. The first step suggests that firms must first identify (or determine) the true needs and wants of its targeted group. To find out the needs and wants of the consumer implies firms must ask consumers. This is generally the task of marketing research — to gather information from consumers as to their needs, wants, likes, beliefs, desires, etc. Generally, marketing research becomes more important in many firms as they become more marketing-oriented. The second step suggests that once a firm has gathered this information, they utilize it to develop the products and services that will satisfy the consumers' needs and wants more effectively than the competition. In today's intensely competitive environment, firms recognize that they must stay informed of their consumers' changing needs and wants and be ready to modify their offerings to keep up with these changes. The era of focusing on product or sales can no longer "cut it" in today's changing marketplace.

Churches: Production-Oriented vs Marketing-Oriented

As mentioned previously, many church leaders are somewhat reluctant to consider proven marketing techniques or concepts in an attempt to satisfy the spiritual needs of their desired publics. They believe that they offer a solid program of worship, prayer, counseling, and preaching which has drawn people in the past and will continue to attract people to these "proven" ministries.

This production approach to ministry is based on the belief that basically persons and society do not change all that much, at least in terms of their spiritual needs, so it is logical to continue offering the same ministry product that has worked so well in the past. The old adage, "If it ain't broke, don't fix it," summarizes the production orientation mentality of many church leaders.

Furthermore, such a belief implies that since the basic ministry "product" remains the same, the church can only get better and better at producing it. In essence, by continuing to strive for improvements in the basic ministry product, the church will continue to attract those in search of what they are offering.

Unfortunately, most of America's churches remain production-oriented churches. Many have been in existence for many genera tions, and the sons and daughters of the church's members have traditionally followed the path of their parents. Family tradition and denominational ties were very strong. For decades, such an approach worked well enough for most churches. As our population increased, most churches either maintained their membership or actually grew as the children raised within a religious family would generally fit very nicely into a conformist, pro-religious culture.

However, there are several, unsettling trends in society that are greatly impacting churches and, as a result, making the production orientation very outdated. To being with, most adults in this country do not regularly attend church worship services. William Easum states:

> Of all the changes affecting the ministry of churches, none is more important than the relationship between the church and culture. The marriage between American culture and Christianity is coming to an end. What was once a separation is becoming a divorce. Not only is the marriage dissolving, but there are signs of actual hostility between the church and society. We are the first generation to live in an unchurched culture. People no longer attend church unless they are shown why they should attend.[1]

Based on his research on churches, George Barna similarly found that since 1976, there has been no appreciable change in the proportion of adults who attend services at any time during the week. This is true in spite of a growing number of churches, increased church spending for advertising and promotion, and the availability of more sophisticated techniques for informing people of a church's existence. In addition, he determined that the average Protestant congregation in this country has 50 to 60 adults who regularly attend Sunday morning worship services. He believes that that is often not enough people for a church to prosper — emotionally, financially, and in many cases, spiritually. Finally, his attitudinal studies have shown that despite a growing public interest in religion, people's confidence in the church as an institution is declining. Furthermore, only a minority of American adults consider the Christian Church to be "relevant for today."[2]

Of great importance for all churches should be the unprecedented abandonment of churches by baby boomers — the generation of Americans born between 1946 and 1964. In the previous two decades, most boomers lost their religion and abandoned their churches. Ironically, most baby boomers began life in religious households. Virtually all (96%) said they were raised in a religious tradition. They attended Sunday schools and religious classes in record numbers and they often were the reasons their parents returned to church. The "religious revival" of the 1950s was due in large part to parents' concerns about the religious education of their children.

However, these baby boomers usually dropped out of church as soon as they could. Most (58%) of those with a religious background dropped out for at least the years during their adolescence or young adulthood. Eighty-four percent of Jews dropped out, as did 60% of mainline Protestants, 57% of Catholics, and 54% of conservative Protestants. Young people have abandoned their churches and temples in the past, but rarely in such large numbers.[3]

Clearly, times are changing for churches as they will continue to face unparalled challenges. Such drastic attitudinal and behavioral shifts necessitate that churches, like other profit and nonprofit organizations, must become more marketing-oriented in order to survive. This implies that churches can no longer rely on their past successes to guarantee growth in the future. What worked so well in the past may be totally inappropriate for today's rapidly changing society.

For a church, a marketing orientation suggests that church leaders first try to determine the spiritual, emotional, relational, etc., needs and wants of that segment of the population it is trying to reach. This implies that a church should have a clear vision as to which segments of the population it intends to pursue. As stated previously, a church today cannot be all things to all people. In other sectors of society, the successful marketers are "niche marketers," implying they target a particular segment of the population, not everyone in general.

Once a church can segment the population and determine who their target market is, they can then proceed to collect information on data about this desired group's needs and then determine what it will take to satisfy these needs. This approach enhances a true "consumer orientation" in which it focuses on the needs of the individual rather than the needs of the church.

Based on his research, Barna found that the churches making a difference in their communities and attracting more and more people are marketing-oriented. He found numerous examples of authentic, Christ-serving churches that use marketing without apology. They proclaim the gospel, they facilitate relationships among people, they serve the community and they do basic marketing activities to enable such ministry to continue and to flourish.[4]

The decision facing churches is clear. They can continue to operate as they have in the past — putting out their ministry product, hoping that it will attract those seeking a relationship with God and a church home. Or they can take the initiative to find out what certain types of people are looking for in a church and decide whether they can provide the type of ministry that can best address these issues — in essence, believing that the ministry of the church exists to serve the needs and interests of their people. Since people's attitudes and behaviors are changing, the church must be aware of these changes and adapt its ministry offerings, while remaining faithful to its doctrine.

The 4 P's of Church Marketing

As stated previously, a marketing orientation is comprised of two basic steps. First, identify the needs and wants of a target market. This is the task of market research, which will be discussed in Chapter 4. Second, based on the collected information, develop the product/service that most efficiently and effectively satisfies these needs and wants.

In attempting to satisfy identified needs and wants, marketers utilize what is often referred to as a marketing mix — those controllable variables which the organization combines and manipulates. These controllable variables are often labelled the 4 P's of marketing. The *product* could involve a physical item and/or some combination of services. *Place* is concerned with the where, when, and by whom the goods are offered for sale. *Promotion* is any method of communication to the target market that the product/service is to be offered for sale. Lastly, *price* is the final component that rounds out the marketing mix and makes it as attractive to the target market as possible, while still providing fair and recommended return to the organization (see Figure 2.1).

In suggesting that churches become more marketing-oriented, it is equally important to discuss the 4 P's of a church's marketing mix that embodies such an orientation. Even though churches do not exist to sell a tangible product or to make a financial profit, they are still involved with the development of a marketing mix.

Product

In regards to a church's "product," it is obviously nothing tangible that its constituents can receive. A church is not trying to sell

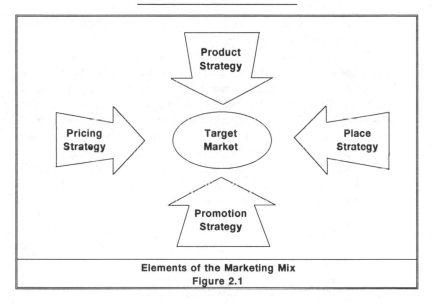

Elements of the Marketing Mix
Figure 2.1

"Jesus" or sell the "Bible." Rather, a church is offering its members a collection of various offerings that might include the various ministries offered by the church: the worship service, outreach programs, bible classes, counseling, preaching, teaching, etc. In essence, a church is actually providing a variety of different products, all of which are more controlled by the members than by the church itself.

Similarly, there may be several intangible aspects of the product that churches provide for its users. Such aspects as a sense of community, a sense of belonging, spiritual guidance, reflection, meditation, a sense of hope, and a sense of purpose to life may be part of the product package. Obviously, these aspects will be perceived differently by a church's members, as well as their relative importance.

Another aspect of the church product is the offering of relationships. Foremost, the church is encouraging its members to develop a lifelong relationship with Jesus Christ. The teachings, encouragements, bible classes, preaching, etc., all help strengthen an individual's personal relationship with God. Secondly, the church is also offering a relationship with others in a church. Again, the interpersonal relationships within a church can provide support, encouragement, friendship, and a sharing of thoughts and ideas that can be so important to many church members. The development of relationships with others in the church can also help further develop one's own relationship with God.

It is obvious that trying to define the "product" in a church marketing mix is a difficult task. The product that is offered is actually many different products, many of which are intangible. Likewise, not all members will view the various product offerings in the same light, and different members will seek out different aspects of the product that best satisfy their own spiritual and emotional needs. The important thing for churches is that they are aware of their members' needs and wants, and that they try to provide the types of product offerings that best fulfill these requirements.

Place

Regarding the P of place, many people may perceive a church as being limited to whatever takes place on the church grounds. In essence, by equating place with the physical location of the church, this results in a very narrow-minded perspective of what this controllable variable actually conveys.

Perhaps a more feasible perspective of the place variable would be to examine how a church "distributes" its product offerings to its desired constituents. In moving beyond simply where the products of a church are offered, i.e., the church facilities, this allows a church to focus on *how* it goes about satisfying the needs and wants of its targeted group. The important consideration is to view the place variable without geographic or physical boundaries.

In distributing the product offering to their various publics, a church may utilize several different vehicles to ensure the needs and wants are satisfied. Some of the church's products, such as preaching, worship services and social interactions, may take place on the church grounds. Other aspects of the product, such as counseling, education, outreach programs, and other ministries may take place in people's homes or out in the community.

Many successful churches have moved beyond the boundaries of the church grounds by encouraging a sense of intimacy among members by breaking the church into smaller units: small group bible classes and kinship groups, where small groups of members meet regularly at someone's house and worship together, support and encourage one another, and help one another develop a closer relationship to God; or social activities such as church-sponsored softball teams, youth groups, singles clubs, etc.

While not to diminish the importance of characteristics of the church facilities, such as location, atmosphere, party facilities, comfort, and safety, the most important aspects of the place decision may involve those activities that often take place outside the church grounds which often are more directly involved in addressing the individual needs and wants of each church member. Whenever relationships are being forged, individuals supported or encouraged or being brought closer to God, this represents the actual "place" of church marketing.

Price

Unlike profit-oriented firms that receive monetary compensation for their product or service, the "price" of church marketing is somewhat more complex. Most assuredly, churches depend on the financial support of their members and couldn't survive without these resources. However, in addition to members' financial support, churches depend very much on members' commitments of time, energy, support, and participation in various activities which ultimately help the church thrive and prosper.

Financial support is not enough. While not to underestimate its importance, churches are constantly faced with a shortage of time and personnel to fully provide the types of services and programs that they try to offer to members and perhaps to the entire community. Even the smallest church needs individuals to teach Sunday school, sing in the choir, serve on various church committees, and perhaps even assist in the maintenance and upkeep of the church facilities.

Larger churches that provide a myriad of programs to the community, such as food parties, outreach programs, recreation programs, etc., also greatly depend on their members' willingness to serve in their own way and help facilitate the implementation and execution of these activities.

Obviously, if an individual perceives his or her spiritual needs being met by the church, then they will most likely be willing to help in some manner on church-related activities, as well as willingly contributing financially to the church. On the other hand, if a church is not addressing the needs of an individual, this person will most likely find convenient excuses not to help in church activities and may only begrudgingly contribute financially.

I believe the marketing concept is inherent in churches getting the most from their members. Again, if the church is sensitive to its members' needs and wants and tries to offer those programs, worships, offerings, etc., to best satisfy these needs and wants, then it will see the benefits not only in the collection plate, but also with an enthusiastic, willing, caring group of members who can greatly aid the church in accomplishing its goals.

Similarly, in trying to attract others in the community, a church must be aware of the specific needs and wants of the segment it is trying to attract. When asked why they don't attend church, many unchurched people claim first, the church is not relevant to them and secondly, the church is always asking for money. The huge segment of baby boomers who remain unchurched represent a great potential for churches in the 90s. Yet, churches must come to grips with the somewhat unique characteristics of this generation and try to understand why they left organized religion. Only when these needs can be identified can churches expect to be able to design the types of offerings that might attract this lost generation back to the church. Baby boomers are not very good belongers, but are great participants. If some of this generation began to find the church more relevant and attuned to their needs, then churches will receive the commitment, both in time and money, to keep them alive and prospering.

Basically, trying to coerce members to increase their financial pledge or trying to strong-arm someone into serving on a church committee or teach Sunday school will not be effective if the church is not doing its job in addressing the true needs and wants of its constituents. The "price" in church marketing includes both time and money, but these variables are entirely dependent on how well the church has satisfied its constituents.

Promotion

Promotion implies communication about the product or service that is being offered. Promotional elements designed to communicate the desired message to the target market can include advertising, publicity, personal selling, sales promotion, and word of mouth.

Regardless of which promotional element(s) are used, the key consideration, once again, is for a church to clearly know what segment of the population it is trying to reach. If their communication attempts are going to be successful, they must use those promotional strategies which are most effective in getting through to the desired segment.

While Chapter 6 discusses the pros and cons of various promotional strategies for churches, research consistently shows that the best form of promotion is word-of-mouth, one-on-one, human interaction. Less than 1% of the "born again" believers in America have committed to a church as a result of watching evangelistic television. Similarly, few have gained as a result of evangelistic magazines, books, or radio programs.[5]

As one of the big aspects of the product of the church is the offering of relationships with others, it is logical that the best way to promote the church is through the development and growth of meaningful relationships with others. Obviously, if members of a church perceive the relationships with others in the church as being supportive and meaningful and also believe their personal relationship with God is being strengthened, then one can assume that these individuals would be more likely to invite their friends and neighbors to attend church with them and hopefully enjoy the same benefits they find so important. Many unchurched people, when asked if they would attend a church service, said they would if someone they knew invited them. It is apparent that if members are satisfied with the "product" offered by their church, they are certainly more apt to consider inviting others, who may only be waiting for an invitation to attend.

Implications for a Marketing-Oriented Church

For a marketing-oriented church, it is imperative that they have a clear understanding of what type of person they are trying to attract. Are they trying to reach people of a certain age group, families, singles, certain lifestyles, those who live near the church, etc.? In essence, the church must have a clear vision as to their desired target market. With family traditions and denominational ties among many people being very weak, it is critical that a church decides on a "niche" they wish to attract.

Having decided upon the segment of society they hope to attract, a church can then proceed with identifying the spiritual and emotional needs and wants of their target market. This task often involves marketing research, and appropriate research strategies for churches will be discussed in Chapter 4. With an identification of the needs, wants, beliefs, desires, attitudes of their chosen segment, they can then begin the task of developing the 4 P's of their marketing mix to produce an attractive "package" that best addresses and hopefully satisfies these issues (see Figure 2.2).

Product
- Relationships
- Worship
- Ministry Offerings
- Sense of Belonging

Place
- Church Facilities
- Beyond the Church

Price
- Financial Contributions
- Time & Effort
- Willingness to Participate

Promotion
Communication:
- Word of Mouth
- Advertising
- Publicity
- Direct Marketing

The 4 P's of Church Marketing
Figure 2.2

If a church has chosen a segment of society that it can best serve and is appropriate for the type of church it is, and has done a sound job in identifying the needs and wants of this segment, then the marketing mix developed should combine the 4 P's in such a way that they are interrelated and logically flow from one to another.

In essence, the successful marketing-oriented church, by identifying the key concerns of its desired publics, will design the types of programs, worships, preaching, counseling, and relationships that their constituents are seeking (product). These product attributes, if appropriate for the target market, can be distributed wherever it is feasible — either on church ground, members' homes, or simply out in the community. The development of strengthening relationships with others and individually with God have no geographic or physical boundaries (place). If an individual perceives his/her spiritual and relational needs are being met by what the church provides, then this person is more likely to be willing to be an active participant in church activities, not only contributing financially, but also with their time, effort, talents, and prayers, to help the church grow and prosper (price). Similarly, the person who believes his/her needs are being met by the church, and who is enjoying the relationships with others in the church, will also be more likely to tell others about the church and even encourage and invite others to come to visit (promotion). Ultimately, this satisfied person can become a marketer for the church, provide an extremely effective way to promote what the church is offering, and help the church face the challenging times ahead.

Endnotes

1. Easum, William, *How to Reach Baby Boomers*, Nashville, TN: Abingdon Press, 1991, p. 18.

2. George Barna, *Marketing the Church*, Colorado Springs, Colorado: Navpress, 1982, pp. 21-22.

3. Wade Roof Clark, "The Baby Boomer's Search for God," *American Demographics*, December 1992, p. 54.

4. George Barna, *Church Marketing*, Ventura, CA: Regal Books, 1992, p. 28.

5. George Barna, *Marketing the Church*, p. 53.

3

Market Segmentation for Churches

Rationale for Church Market Segmentation

In previous times churches did not have to worry so much about attracting new members to keep its vitality. Members' children, strong on tradition and denominational loyalty, could be counted on to continue a family's local religious tradition. Since churches could depend on such a "feeder" system, this helps explain why so few churches felt the need to become more user-oriented. The production-orientation was again appropriate under these conditions since churches were confident that the types of services, worships, and programs that were offered in the past would be equally well-received by the next generation of church members.

Unfortunately, this comfortable scenario has changed drastically. The pipeline of church members' children is no longer dependable. Baby boomers usually dropped out of church as soon as they could. Many of the baby boomers who dropped out of religion have not returned to church. These religious dropouts claim over one-third of baby boomers, including 34% of those raised as mainline Protestants, 30% of Catholics, and 30% of conservative Protestants.[1]

Such abandonment from the largest segment of the population has left many churches with dwindling membership and resources. As the median age of many church members continues to rise and the lack of any new faces becomes alarming, it is time for churches to become more active in trying to attract new members. The good

---

news is that many of the baby boomers who have abandoned the church are now beginning to become more religious and are searching for a church home. However, what is confusing and frustrating to churches today is that those turning to religion again demonstrate very little denominational loyalty. Many of this generation believe that one should "explore many different religious traditions" rather than "stick to a particular faith."[2] In essence, those returnees are "shopping" for a church home, sampling various faiths, types of worships, social activities and church programs, trying to find the type of church that best addresses their needs.

As our population becomes more and more diverse, it is apparent that no church can be all things to all people. The "mass marketing" approach that seemed very appropriate a generation ago for churches is no longer feasible. No single marketing mix designed by a church can attract everyone. In addition, since so many churches face dwindling funds, they must be extremely careful in allocating these precious resources in trying to attract new members. Trying to attract or satisfy everyone in a community may result in no one's needs being met and may doom the church marketer's efforts to failure.

Like so many other profit and nonprofit firms, churches need to fully realize that their marketing efforts need to be directed at specific market segments. Before a marketing mix can be implemented, church leaders must identify, evaluate, and select a target market. The time is now for churches to embrace the concept of market segmentation, which is the process of dividing the total market into relatively homogeneous groups. For churches, this will require their leaders to first identify factors that affect participation in membership decisions so that people can be grouped accordingly. The marketing mix of the church can then be adjusted to meet the needs of each targeted segment.

Bases of Segmentation

If a local church has decided that a "mass marketing" approach is no longer effective in attracting new members, then it faces the difficult decisions of how to best segment the population and secondly, which segment or segments it should pursue. The problem is thus twofold. First, select one of the many different bases of segmentation that have been identified and utilized by other marketers.

Second, to decide among three basic strategies: whether to pursue one segment of the population (concentrated approach); to pursue several segments of the population, each requiring a unique marketing mix (differentiated approach); or to treat the entire market as their target — in essence continue practicing "mass marketing" (undifferentiated approach).

There are many ways in which a given market can be segmented. The bottom line is that there is not one right/best way to segment the population. A church that desires to utilize a segmentation approach needs to evaluate the potential bases for segmentation and select the one most appropriate for its purposes. A segmentation base is optimal if it yields segments possessing the following characteristics: (1) "mutual exclusivity" — each segment should be conceptually separable from all other segments; (2) "exhaustiveness" — every potential target market should be included in some segment; (3) "measurability" — the segment size and profile can be readily measured; (4) "accessibility" — the resulting segments can be effectively reached and served; (5) "substantiability" — the degree to which the resulting segments are large enough to be worth pursuing; (6) "differential responsiveness" — the degree to which each segment responds to different offerings and marketing program.[3]

With these criteria in mind, a church should look at the bases of segmentation often utilized by other marketers (Exhibit 3.1). To begin with, the easiest way to segment a market is "geographically." By putting the church on a map and drawing circles with a one-mile, three-mile, or five-mile radius, it is possible to estimate how many people live within that driving time. While some people may be willing to drive long distances to attend their desired church, geographic segmentation provides a reasonable assessment of the market potential for a local church. Similarly, churches may identify a particular zip code in their geographic target market. This provides a convenient boundary within which they are trying to meet the needs of the local community.

Probably the most common base of segmentation is to break down a population on a demographic variable such as age, sex, family size, income, occupation, family lifecycle, or religion. By segmenting the market with a demographic variable, it is possible to better understand the "type" of people in the population. Again, the difficult decision for the church, if it chooses demographic segmentation, is which demographic variable is most appropriate for their

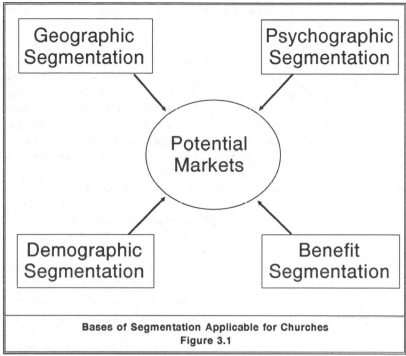

Bases of Segmentation Applicable for Churches
Figure 3.1

purpose. The key advantage of demographic segmentation is that these variables, are generally easier to measure than other variables, and marketers often find that a person's wants and preferences are often highly associated with demographic variables. A church could obtain such information from census data, or perhaps from local newspaper offices which collect such information for advertising purposes.

Segmenting the population based on age is a logical base of segmentation. People's needs and wants obviously change with age. Churches may offer various types of programs or activities for children, teenagers, young adults, seniors, etc. The availability of youth groups or senior citizen clubs may be of special interest to those age groups and may provide a type of fulfillment that is lacking in their lives.

Similarly, segmenting people on their marital status represents another logical base. For years, most churches have focused much of their efforts on families — married couples, generally with children. Much of the churches' programs, activities, and plans were directed at the traditional American family. Again, times have changed.

Demographics have confirmed that the singles population in the United States is in excess of 50% of all adults above the age of 18. This phenomenon is a new reality for the 1990s. Couples with children will no longer be dominating the pews. Neither will married people represent a majority of the demographics in a church. It is important to realize that the singles segment is very complex, because it represents numerous age categories and lifestyles: teenagers who have left home, single parents in their 20s, divorcees in their 30s with their children, single fathers, the never-married of various ages, as well as the elderly — both widows and widowers.

The new reality of a large and growing singles segment may force churches to face new issues when planning their services, programs, and ministries. Churches can no longer afford to view singles with any bias, and must actually take the necessary steps to fully involve and integrate singles into the life and ministry of the church.

Of special interest to church leaders might also be psychographic segmentation. This term refers to "lifestyle" variables and is based on the notion that "we do what we do because it fits into the kind of life we are living or want to live." Most approaches to identifying lifestyle groups is based on measures of individuals' activities, interests, and opinions (AIOs).

For example, some churches have attempted to emphasize the individual over the institution in trying to attract the "unchurched" baby boomers. Some baby boomers are reluctant to attend the formalized institutions, but feel much more at home in a casual setting. In essence, they are drawn to a church that offers informality with meaning.

Similarly, those searching for a church home that offers informality with meaning may be attracted to a particular congregation that stresses relationships rather than strict adherence to creeds or doctrinal statements. The casual atmosphere, both in terms of dress and worship, and the focusing on developing relationships with others may be highly correlated with an individual's lifestyle.

While psychographic segmentation has helped produce a very thorough descriptor of the target market of hundreds of goals and services, it is a more difficult means of segmentation than geographic or demographic, and as a result might be beyond the reach of some churches. The output of psychographic segmentation results in lifestyle profiles developed from asking respondents to agree or disagree with AIO statements, which are often a collection of several hundred statements dealing with activities, interests, and opinions. This process would involve a sophisticated marketing research design in which the costs and expertise required for developing the survey, administering it to the desired sample, and analyzing the data might be beyond the financial and staff resources of most churches. Still, it is a proven technique and is a good addition to segmentation done by demographic or geographic variables.

Finally, another appropriate base would be behavioral segmentation in which individuals are segmented based on their knowledge, attitude, use, or response to churches. For example, people could be segmented based on the benefits they seek from exchanges with the church. Church members may not be seeking the same benefits or place the same importance on each benefit. Marketing research conducted by the church could identify what the various internal and external markets are seeking. Similarly, church members could be categorized based on their attendance rate (light, medium, heavy), on their loyalty status (none, medium, strong, absolute), etc. Behavioral segmentation could prove very useful to churches who are seeking to identify and understand how and why certain congregations are selected by people on different market segments to satisfy some of their needs.

Again, behavioral segmentation is a more sophisticated and costly approach than geographic and demographic, since it also would require marketing research to identify the benefits individuals are seeking, their level of attendance, or other behavioral characteristics. While not as complex as psychographic segmentation, behavioral segmentation would still require the financial resources and expertise to conduct thorough research to elicit the desired responses.

Regardless of which base of segmentation is selected, the key factor is that the church recognizes that different groups exist and not everyone's needs are the same. While the various bases of segmentation differ in terms of their complexity and cost, it is imperative that churches desiring to segment their market (or members of the congregation) select a base that addresses their cost and staff constraints and yet still allows the church leaders to choose their target market more accurately.

Segmentation Strategies

Having selected a base of segmentation appropriate for a particular church, the next task for the church marketer is to make the critical decision as to which segment(s) they should pursue. Segmentation merely reveals the market segment opportunities facing the church; they must select a suitable strategy that will best match the church's offerings to the needs of the chosen target market(s). The three basic target market strategies are undifferentiated marketing, concentrated marketing, and differentiated marketing.

If a church pursues an "undifferentiated" marketing strategy, it is, in essence, ignoring the different segments that make up the market. It is, instead, trying to focus on the similarities of the individual's needs, rather than their differences. The church is basically continuing a "mass marketing" approach in that it has designed a basic offering or program that they hope will appeal to the broadest number of people. This might be exemplified by a church that has one basic weekend service for everyone. Some churches may select this strategy based on extremely limited resources, claiming they cannot afford to differentiate or try to appeal to different groups. Similarly, church leaders may view their immediate market as being quite homogeneous in its needs and desires, implying that little would be gained by differentiated offerings. However, the author believes that such a viewpoint is narrow-minded and ignores all the changes in our population and society.

In rejecting the "mass marketing" mindset, some churches may decide to pursue a "concentrated" marketing strategy. This implies that after breaking down the population into distinct and meaningful segments, it chooses to pursue one segment and designs its programs and offerings to attract that particular target market. The advantage of such an approach is that this provides a better understanding of the needs and desires of the particular segment, and the church, by focusing on only this segment, can better design the types of programs and offerings to satisfy them more effectively than other churches. However, the risk is that the church is, in essence, "putting all its eggs in one basket." If the target segment is declining in number or nonresponsive to the church's efforts, the church leaders may have to rethink their strategy and perhaps shift their focus to other segment(s).

Finally, a third strategy would be for a church to follow a "differentiated" marketing approach. This implies that after the church has segmented the market, it identifies two or more of these segments to pursue with the intention of designing unique ministries and offerings to each segment. By offering ministry and marketing variations, it hopes to attain a higher number of exchanges and a deeper position within each market segment. However, the disadvantage of this approach is that it is the most expensive strategy. Each segment pursued will require its unique marketing mix. Some religious organizations may actually push the differentiated approach too far in that they offer more segmented programs than are economically feasible. George Barna, in identifying key characteristics of growing churches, determined that these churches recognized the numerous opportunities for addressing needs in the community, but they restricted their outreach to those ministries for which they had sufficient resources to do an outstanding job. They saw their decision as a means of maximizing their influence, doing their own ministries superbly, providing evidence of the effectiveness of church, and establishing new opportunities to tell people that the impressive work of the church is a reflection of God's leading and blessing. They also believed that if every church were to assume this attitude, the many existing needs of the population would be addressed by the entire church community, instead of a relative handful of churches.[4]

Examples of Church Market Segmentation

Most marketers contend that American society can no longer be effectively reached through mass marketing. As stated previously, successful marketers these days have found their "niche" — targeting a particular segment of the population, not everyone in general. The same message is true for churches. If a church is going to be successful in the 90s, it cannot treat people as if they constitute a single, massive, undifferentiated audience. Rather, it must respond to people personally as individuals. It must recognize the differences existing, and then segment the population in such a way to determine the appropriate target market and determine what it will take to satisfy their needs.

In addition, market segmentation can enable a church to specialize and achieve excellence in ministry rather than being spread too thin and accomplishing very little. It can also enable a church too more wisely allocate its scarce resources and receive the greatest impact from these expenditures.

Fortunately, several marketing-oriented churches have been quite successful in utilizing a market segmentation approach which has allowed them to grow and attract new members from their selected target market. Willow Creek Community Church in South Barrington, Illinois is often used as a successful model for many "mega-churches" whose congregations number in the thousands. Pastor Bill Hybels began Willow Creek in 1975 by asking a door-to-door sample of local people why they didn't attend church and then what they would want in a church. Hybels' target market was basically the "unchurched." Based on the responses he received, Hybels has tried to give unchurched people all of what they want and nothing they don't want.

Most importantly, Hybels and Willow Creek understand market segmentation. A brochure given to first-time visitors outlines a range of different programs for children, teenagers, older singles, adults, elderly people, and people who are in the midst of a personal crisis. Within the singles program are "Primetime," a social and prayer group for 18 to 32-year-olds, "Focus," for older baby boomers, "Quest," for older singles, and "Grasp" for single parent families.[5]

Such a market segmentation approach has been extremely beneficial for Willow Creek since it attracts about 14,000 to its entertainment-oriented weekend services and 5,000 "true believers" to its more religious Wednesday evening services.

George Barna describes the success of one congregation which, after employing a segmentation approach, grew from a handful of people to several hundred within three years. They did so without a ministry for children and teens. This was not because they saw no need of such a ministry. They planned to launch this ministry, but only when they knew what they were doing, and were assured they would do it with excellence. "The last thing I want to do is drive those parents and their kids out of here because we weren't really ready to deal with them," the pastor said. "Once we have our act together, we'll launch our youth ministry. Until then, I'd be doing this church and those families a disservice by allowing us to offer a half-baked, premature outreach."[6]

When the church did launch the youth and children's program six months later, it was instrumental in ushering in more than 200 new members within six months.

Another successful mega-church is Saddleback Community Church which has started 20 "sister" congregations, each planning its own program to fit the particular needs and interests of its congregations and community. This is in contrast to structuring the churches so that they would all be carrying out identical programs. A local church may select specific census data or zip codes in which to operate within a geographic area.[7]

Another example of a successful segmentation approach was exemplified by Alan Houghton who stated: "Churches sometimes forget who the customers are." A Harvard MBA, Houghton became rector of Manhattan's Church of the Heavenly Rest, a then weak parish. By the time he left nine years later, the church's once shrinking endowment was growing steadily and average attendance quadrupled.

Houghton's secret was to find a need the competition wasn't meeting. "In New York City, churches are like restaurants — there is one on every block," he said. "If you don't like the menu, you can walk down the street to eat somewhere else. We decided to try being a family parish in the middle of New York." He put a heavy emphasis on pastoral counseling, encouraged parents to push their infant's carriages in the aisles, and he and his fellow priests greeted parishioners outside the building before services.[8]

The preceding examples all illustrate the importance for a church to find its niche. No church can be all things to all people. Those churches that desire to attract new members and grow need to understand that different population segments respond to different ministry opportunities and focusing one's marketing efforts on a target group allows for a more efficient attraction of that market. The previously discussed successes illustrate that targeting a church's limited resources to reach a specific segment of the population will enable their ministry to be more effective than if they attempted to reach every group in the community and meet the needs of every person in the community.

Implications

As many church memberships continue to decline, appropriate actions will be needed to reverse the trend. If churches are willing to become more marketing-oriented, then they must also realize that there have been drastic shifts in attitudes, behaviors, and loyalties towards churches. Today's church cannot be all things to all people. Instead, they must be aware of their benefits and focus on the segment of society whose spiritual needs they believe they can effectively satisfy.

Those churches often cited as models of growing, successful congregations tend to be the ones already employing "niche" marketing. They've successfully segmented the market into distinct and meaningful groups, chosen the appropriate segment(s) to pursue, and have designed their offerings and services to most effectively satisfy their target market. There are an estimated 70 million "unchurched" Americans. I believe that those churches that begin to understand and implement segmentation strategies will be more successful in attracting new members than those churches who naively continue to follow a mass marketing "shotgun" approach. Obviously, market segmentation has been widely used in the for-profit sector and for many nonprofit organizations. It is time for churches to consider using this proven technique to ensure their growth and prosperity in the future.

Endnotes

1. Wade Clark Roof, "The Baby Boomers Search for God," *American Demographics,* December 1992, p. 55.

2. *Ibid.,* p. 54.

3. Norman Shawchuck, Philip Kotler, Bruce Wrenn, and Gustave Roth, *Marketing for Congregations,* Nashville, TN: Abingdon Press, 1992, p. 173-74.

4. George Barna, *User Friendly Churches,* Ventura CA: Regal Books, 1991, p. 56.

5. Deidre Sullivan, "Targeting Souls," *American Demographics,* October, 1991, p. 44.

6. Barna, *op. cit.,* p. 56.

7. Shawchuck, *op. cit.,* p. 79.

8. Thomas Stewart, "Turning Around the Lord's Business," *Fortune,* Sept. 25, 1989, p.

4

Marketing Research for Churches

Introduction

All firms need accurate and timely information in order to make effective decisions. Likewise, firms need mechanisms to analyze this information and be able to efficiently communicate this information to the relevant decision-makers. Churches are no different from any other firm in that they also need to know what information they need, where to find it, and how to use it once they've obtained it.

If a firm is marketing-oriented, this implies that it is trying to identify the needs and wants of its target market and then adapt itself to delivering the desired satisfaction more effectively and efficiently than the competitors. Marketing research embodies the first half of the marketing orientation. If a firm wants to identify its desired segment's needs and wants, then it must go and obtain this information, and that is the main job of marketing research. Only after the pertinent information has been gathered and analyzed should a firm then develop the types of products or services to satisfy its selected target market.

Unfortunately, many tend to overestimate the value and potential of marketing research. In essence, marketing research is a tool — designed for the systematic gathering and analyzing of information for the purpose of improving the effectiveness of decision-making. It is not the decision that an organization makes. It is not the evaluation of decisions. Research is nothing magical. By itself it cannot turn around a sinking ship — it can't increase sales, profits, market share, etc. If properly designed, a marketing research project can obtain the needed information or data that, when analyzed, can enhance the firm's decision-making process that might ultimately effect sales profits, or market share.

Some organizations decide to "try" marketing research when conditions become perilous. They view research as a last resort to stem falling sales, profits, etc. By itself, marketing research cannot stop such calamities. A few years ago, I was invited in by a local transit manager to conduct some research for his organization. They had decided it was time to do some marketing research because ridership had been declining and they wanted something done to reverse the trend. The troubled manager wasn't exactly sure what information was needed, or who it should be collected from, and was even unsure as to how the collected information should be utilized. I spent a great deal of time discussing similar projects I had conducted for other transit firms, such as collecting data from riders on their likes, dislikes, opinions, etc., or collecting data from the served community, focusing on the opinions, attitudes, intentions, etc., of non-riders as well as riders. I also tried to inform this individual on the limitations of research — describing it as a tool to gather the information they deemed pertinent. The transit manager seemed to listen intently to my presentation, and then proclaimed that he would hire me to conduct some research only if I would guarantee that ridership would go up. I tried to calmly explain that there was no way I could guarantee such a turnaround in ridership. Again, I tried various ideas, such as surveying non-riders, to see if the firm could do anything to encourage some of these individuals to leave their cars at home and try commuting by bus. He listened to my proposals, but adamantly insisted upon a guarantee for ridership to increase. After a few more attempts to define the purpose of marketing research, and with the transit manager firmly insisting upon a written guarantee in the contract for ridership to increase, our meeting came to an end. I obviously did *not* get the contract. It is obvious that firms attempting to conduct some marketing research need to be aware not only of what they can expect from the project, but also what the limitations of research are.

Churches that consider utilizing marketing research, whether to determine the needs and wants of its members, as a means to better serve the congregation, or perhaps to survey the needs and wants of those individuals in their community in an attempt to determine what they might be able to do to attract some of the community to their church, need to clearly understand the benefits of research as well as the limitations, cost, and time of the project. There are many churches today that are having trouble attracting new members and are locking themselves into a pattern of gradual decline. For such a church to survive, it must not only attract new members, but also continue to satisfy and maintain their present members. Marketing research becomes essential in any industry when customers are hard to find and hard to understand. Religion is no different, and a growing number of churches have begun to utilize marketing research in an attempt to understand the needs of unchurched Americans and hopefully attract them back to the fold.

Common Objections Towards Marketing Research

Since some church leaders still have a basic mistrust toward the very nature of marketing and firmly believe the concept as being inappropriate for churches, it is not surprising that several common objections towards the use of marketing research have been quickly adopted by some church leaders which have prevented many churches from conducting any type of marketing research.

While there exist many misconceptions over what marketing research can accomplish for an organization, there also are many misconceptions as to what marketing research involves or implies for the organization. In their classic book on strategy for nonprofit organizations, Kotler and Andreasen identify five myths that have resulted in nonprofit organizations doing insufficient research.[1]

- big decision only
- survey myopia
- "big bucks"
- sophisticated researcher
- research is not read

The "big decision only" myth implies that some religious leaders who are at least open to the use of marketing research may consider doing some only for decisions where large financial invest ments are at stake. This myth implies that research should only be conducted if there is going to be a major capital improvement planned or a major expenditure for a new program. Conversely, this myth also infers that research should only be conducted if the church is facing major problems — dramatic decline in membership, extreme financial difficulties, unrest among the members, etc.

Very similarly, marketing research costs commonly consist of two types — the expense incurred from doing the research itself, and the costs incurred in delaying a decision until the results are available. The benefits in doing a cost/benefit analysis consist of improved decision-making based on the research results. On the other hand, the cost/benefit ratio may sometimes come out against doing the research, even when the stakes are high. Conversely, research can often be justified even when the stakes are low. Such is the case whenever the research is minimal, takes little time, and will ultimately help clarify the decisions to be made. It is obvious that church leaders need to be aware of the costs of research, especially some of the low-cost research techniques; but more importantly, they must assess the potential benefits of the research in order to evaluate whether the research could prove useful.

Another myth of marketing research shared by many, not just church leaders, is that marketing research requires a survey to obtain the desired information. Similarly, a survey implies complex samples, plans, sophisticated data analysis and statistics and would involve large costs. After identifying the pertinent information needed, there is a tendency to jump right into designing a survey to obtain the data. This tendency is understandable since a survey is the most common method of generating primary data. Similarly, we have all been exposed to collecting information from surveys, whether by someone mailing surveys to our house, calling us to ask a few questions about a particular product/service, or having an individual, with placard in hand, stop us in a mall to ask a few questions. Or we have seen the results of surveys conducted by Gallup, Harris, CNN, ABC polls, etc. We have all seen the results of political polls, or public opinion polls conducted by these organizations.

While surveys are the most common way to obtain primary data, there are other research methods that might be more appropriate for certain studies and also may involve substantially smaller costs. There are several simple research methods that can be highly effective for churches and obtain the desired information without the cost and complexity of designing a survey. In essence, church leaders need to become aware of the alternatives to obtaining the needed information, and be able to select the most appropriate methods depending on the objectives of the study, the available data, the urgency of the decision, and the costs of obtaining the data. Traditional survey research definitely has its time and place, but church leaders must know how and when to use some of the alternative low-cost techniques. In a later section, these low-cost techniques will be discussed, since many religious organizations typically operate on restricted budgets.

Analogous to the "big decision only" myth is the "big bucks" myth. Here the belief is that marketing research will always involve big costs. Such a misconception must be very inhibiting to many church leaders where there is often very little budgeted to sustain any kind of marketing research effort.

George Barna contends that since many churches do not have much of a marketing budget, some church leaders believe there is no sense in even considering marketing research.[2] In addition, pastors go to seminary, not MBA programs. They have no training in marketing research, and as a result, may view any type of marketing research as being quite complex and most definitely expensive. While marketing research can certainly be complex and expensive, church leaders may find that for some of their needed information, the data is easily and inexpensively obtainable and a simple research method may be the most feasible.

Just as some church leaders may be wary of the perceived costs of marketing research, others are very inhibited by the perceived complexity and sophistication implied by a majority of research projects. Pick up any undergraduate marketing research textbook and there will be sections of sophisticated sampling techniques, multivariate statistics, computer analyses, etc. Such topics could be very unnerving to the church leader considering marketing research. Again, while some projects may require a high level of sophistication and involve elaborate research designs, there are many times a simple research method can be highly effective. Unless the church leader becomes aware of alternative, low-cost research methods, the "sophisticated researcher" myth may also serve as a convenient reason not to conduct any marketing research.

The final myth that research is not read is again a convenient obstacle to not conducting any marketing research. If the researcher does not clearly understand the original information need or if the purpose of the research was unclear, then the results of the project will most likely be somewhat unhelpful. Similarly, if the results of a carefully planned project are ignored because they don't coincide with the user's own opinion or they address a hot, political issue, then the time and cost spent on the project will be a waste. If a church commits to conducting some research, there must be agreement among those involved in the project as to how the collected information will be utilized to improve decision-making. Similarly, the project should be developed in an objective, unbiased manner, without anyone's prejudices, political pressures, or expectations factored in. Sometimes research conducted as "conscience" money may be fully acclaimed and supported if it backs up the belief and contention of the client, but blasted and scorned if it goes against the prevailing belief. Church leaders must agree to accept the results of a research project even if it goes against the grain of how they perceived the issue under study.

The point is that these myths have prevented many nonprofit organizations from even conducting marketing research, or resulted in inappropriate research. It is essential that church leaders become aware that marketing research does not always necessitate a huge budget or always require sophisticated sampling plans or analytical techniques. Furthermore, they must become cognizant that research need not be reserved for only big decision/big financial investment situations.

One of the best examples of a highly effective, single and low-cost research approach involves the classic, door-to-door survey conducted by Bill Hybels, who founded Willow Creek Community Church in South Barrington, Illinois. Hybels' research was quite basic. Eight hours a day, six days a week, he asked, "Do you actively attend a local church?" If the answer was yes, he went on to the next house. If the answer was no, he asked, "Why not?," and charted the responses. Among the most frequent responses were "churches are always asking for money" or "church services are boring, predictable, routine, and irrelevant." When his survey was completed, he knew a lot about the unchurched and he had a list of hundreds of people who said they might come to a church that was different. Willow Creek's first service drew 125 of them. There was no collection and they got "a service for seekers — Christianity 101 and Christianity 201." Now the weekend service attendance is in excess of 15,000. Newcomers hear the church doesn't want their money until they've decided they want the church.

A Marketing Research Process for Churches

Introduction

If church leaders can overcome the common objection to utilizing marketing research in their organizations and can also dispel some of the research myths described in the previous section, then it is appropriate for these leaders to develop a plan for conducting research to help their church more effectively identify both the needs of the congregation and the segment of the population they hope to attract.

The marketing research process implies a series of interrelated steps that logically follow one another. While certainly most marketing research textbooks and handbooks discuss the process, there is no firm agreement as to the exact number of steps or the naming of each of these steps. For this book, the suggested marketing research process will involve a five-step procedure (Figure 4.1).

---

1. Determine Research Purpose
   - Identify Information Needs
   - Set Specific Objectives

   ↓

2. Conduct Exploratory Research
   - Evaluate Secondary Data
   - Conduct Qualitative Research

   ↓

3. Design Formal Research
   - Design Survey
   - Develop Sampling Plan
   - Collect Data

   ↓

4. Perform Data Analysis
   - Tabulate Responses
   - Utilize Appropriate Statistical Techniques (Objective)

   ↓

5. Interpret Data and Develop Recommendations
   - Provide Meaningful Explanation of Data (Subjective)
   - Recommend Specific Actions

The Marketing Research Process for Religious Organizations
Figure 4.1

Determine Research Purpose

The first step in research is to determine the purpose of the research — why is the information being gathered? This is undoubtedly the most critical step of the entire process. If the purpose is vaguely defined, or the wrong purpose addressed, or the intended uses of the information not made clear, then the entire marketing research effort may be misleading or even useless.

Church leaders will need to understand the importance of closely defining the purpose of their intended research. Not only do they need to ask "What information do we need?," but perhaps more importantly, "Why do we need this information?" It is essential that those conducting the research and the ultimate decisions made should attempt to have a clear understanding of the answers to those questions, and both parties need also to agree on the ultimate purpose of undertaking the research. The phrase, "a problem well-defined is a problem half-solved" is very appropriate for researchers. If the purpose of the research is clear, the chances of collecting the pertinent information will be much greater. Likewise, a clearly stated purpose will enhance the development of proper research objectives. After establishing that the research will serve a useful purpose, the next step is to state exactly the research objectives. This statement of research objectives should lead to a listing of specific information requirements. In other words, this stage implies going from the general to the specific. While this early stage may become tedious and difficult to reach closure, the second stage of the suggested research approach — exploratory research — often helps obtain further clarification of the objectives by more clearly illuminating the marketing opportunity or threat.

Exploratory Research

When a researcher has a limited amount of experience with or knowledge about a research issue, exploratory research is a useful preliminary step. It helps ensure that a more rigorous, more conclusive future study will not begin with an inadequate understanding of the nature of the marketing problem.

For churches, exploratory research is a necessary step before committing precious resources towards a more formal research approach. Most churches do not have large budgets set aside for conducting marketing research, nor a staff of highly trained, experienced research analysts. These constraints necessitate that church leaders recognize the need to integrate available, reliable information into its marketing activities and actively pursue that integration. The purpose of the exploratory research process is to progressively narrow the scope of the research topic and transform the discovered problems into defined ones, incorporating specific research objectives. After such exploration, the researcher should know which data to collect during the formal research, and how to conduct the project.[3]

At this stage, church leaders have two basic techniques for obtaining insights and greater clarity of the problem: examining secondary data sources and conducting qualitative research.

Secondary data are data collected by someone else for some other purpose. This brief definition implies that secondary data may not be exactly the information required for a particular project, but still these sources should be evaluated first, prior to moving on to more complex and certainly more expensive survey research. The main advantages of secondary data are that they are generally easily obtainable and often at little or no cost. Certainly, the place to start would be the internal records of the church. All churches maintain some type of information on its members or the community. Any documents, records, news releases, member information sheets, etc., may be helpful in addressing certain information needs. Even if this information isn't exactly what is required, it might be helpful to provide direction, insight, and a greater understanding of the problem at hand.

Aside from internal records, church leaders should avail themselves of other sources of secondary data which might be easily obtainable from local libraries. Conducting a literature search on a particular topic would be extremely helpful and informative and provide the user with an extensive list of what's been written on the topic.

Other sources of secondary data can be obtained from the government. The government publishes several different census as well as special reports on various issues, and again this information can likely be obtained at local libraries.

There are also a growing number of private organizations whose expertise is analyzing and interpreting demographic data. Available at a cost, this data can be extremely focused and manipulated to address specific information needs of a local church. Similarly, an increasing number of organizations are providing information on lifestyles in America and have segmented the population into dozens of different lifestyle segments. Again, by understanding the demographic and lifestyle breakdown of a community, a church desiring to attract new members may be able to utilize this data to better understand the needs and wants of the unchurched residents of the community. One note of caution is that these services could be expensive for some churches, and this implies that the church must have a clear idea as to what specific information is needed and how it will be utilized. A lot of information from secondary data sources may be interesting, but is it really what the church needs for the problem at hand?

Finally, in utilizing secondary data, church leaders need to be aware that since it was data collected by someone else for some other purpose, it may not exactly meet their specific information needs. They also need to be concerned over the timeliness of the data — it may be too outdated for the church's use, the quality of the data — what was the purpose of the original study? An unbiased project or to support someone's vested interest ("conscience money")? They need to know, too, the reliability of the collected data — i.e., was it based on a small sample, who was sampled, how was the data collected?, etc.

Regardless of the inexact fit of most secondary data, it is still a very helpful and necessary step in the research process. It can provide the researcher with a better understanding of the problem at hand and provide a clear focus and direction for the subsequent steps in the process.

As a supplement to gathering appropriate secondary data, church leaders might also benefit from conducting some type of qualitative research in order to gain further insight into the factors playing a role in the marketing problem being investigated. Qualitative research is mainly concerned with understanding "how and why" people think and act, rather than how many people think or act that way. The idea behind qualitative research is to grasp insight into the quality of their thought-out actions; the intensity of feelings, the breadth of understanding, the depth of importance. The methods through which qualitative research are derived emphasize the character of people's beliefs, opinions, attitudes, and values, not simply the basic content of these elements.[4]

Several forms of qualitative research are suitable for churches. To begin with, indepth personal interviews with selected individuals from the desired constituency can provide detailed information on the issues addressed, and again could provide the researcher with additional insight and direction. Indepth interviews are generally informal, unstructured interviews in which the interviewer can ask a variety of questions and probe for elucidation when appropriate. One note of caution is that since indepth interviews are generally one-on-one, they can be extremely time-consuming if many individuals are to be queried. Similarly, the role of the interviewer is crucial — what questions to ask, when to probe for more detail, how to keep the respondent on the topic at hand, etc., are all vital ingredients of a successful interviewer. If the church leader or other members of the church are not comfortable in the role of the interviewer and a professional must be hired, this could be quite an expense for the church.

Another type of qualitative research would be to carry out observations in certain situations. Observation research is extremely limited because the researcher is only able to observe current behavior. The researcher is unable to understand the motivation behind the behavior and also has no clue as to the observant's attitudes, opinions, interests, and demographic information. In certain situations, observation methods might be utilized, assuming the church researcher is cognizant of what to observe, how to properly record the observation, and understands the complex interactions among the constituents and the church system under study.[5] The limitations of observation research, as well as the fact that interpretation of the observer is highly subjective, make it a less desirable means of obtaining information than other types of exploratory research.

Finally, some churches are turning to focus groups to help clarify issues and opportunities. Focus groups are similar to indepth interviews in that they too are unstructured, informal, free-flowing interviews. The main difference is that focus groups generally involve a small group (7-10 people), and the role of the moderator is critical to the success or failure of the focus group. Focus groups allow people to discuss their true feelings, anxieties, and frustrations, as well as the depth of their convictions in their own words. The primary advantages of focus group interviews are that they are relatively fast, easy to execute, and inexpensive.[6] Church leaders considering focus groups need to be aware of the central importance of a good moderator. The moderator's job can be quite difficult in that he/she must know what questions to ask, when to probe for detail, how to ensure all participants are heard, and must possess some understanding of group dynamics. Secondly, it is imperative that those using focus groups do not attempt to finalize its findings. Focus groups are comprised of a small group of people and cannot be considered truly representative of the specified segment. Like other forms of exploratory research, focus group findings should be viewed as a suitable replacement for survey research based on a much larger sample of the desired segment. Instead, these groups should provide a sampling of different opinions, attitudes and ideas that will provide helpful insight and direction into the problem at hand and provide valuable assistance in moving toward more formal research (see Exhibit 4.2).

Focus groups are also often used to help assess different themes in commercials. In 1977, the Baptist General Convention of Texas prepared an extensive marketing campaign to increase membership in its church. As a test, four commercials were shown to separate groups consisting of active Christians, nonactive Christians, and non-Christians. All these segments gave their biggest rating to testimonials in which the speakers indicated how important their faith in Christ had been in overcoming their own problems. In one, the speaker said that he had been a revolutionary, but his life had been changed by another revolutionary, and he closed with the statement: "My name is Eldridge Cleaver. I'm living proof." This "living proof" campaign was later widely used throughout the United States. Focus groups were also used to help set criteria for acceptable spokespersons.[7]

It is evident that the second stage, exploratory research, encompasses a wide range of activities — from collecting available and relatively inexpensive secondary data to setting up much more detailed and expensive focus groups. Regardless of which methods of exploratory research are selected, the purpose should be to provide the church leader with greater insight, clarification, and a sense of direction for the intended research purpose and to specify objectives the research process should entail.

Formal Research

Having specifically defined the purpose of the research and assessing the appropriate exploratory research, church leaders must then decide whether to conduct more formal research. Again, realizing that few churches budget any money for research, it is imperative that church leaders who do wish to proceed with a more structured research design need to evaluate the costs and time requirements involved in designing a survey, developing a sampling plan, and collecting the data.

Based on my consulting with small businesses, I have found many managers grossly underestimate the task of designing a survey. To many, survey design merely implies writing a few questions and then getting a certain number of people to answer them. Trying to be helpful, some clients have presented me with their list of survey questions. On the other hand, many feel that designing a reliable survey is the job of an experienced market researcher. Unless the church has someone in the congregation with expertise in the area, the church should probably consider seeking the assistance of professionals.

Fortunately, or unfortunately, depending on your viewpoint, survey design is not a science, but an art. Marketing research texts generally provide various do's and don't's of question construction. Much of the advice is good common sense, such as: keep the questions brief, make sure they are understandable, avoid complex terminology, don't bias the respondent, ensure the question can be answered, etc.

However, the researcher, even in trying to follow the sage advice given in research textbooks, may still develop questions that cause problems among the respondents. Similar to not being able to see the forest because of trees, the researcher, having written the questions, is expecting a certain response. Many times a researcher is amazed at the variety of responses provided that were totally unexpected. Likewise, the researcher assumes the respondent understands the question, has the knowledge to answer the question, and will answer the question in the proper manner. An experienced researcher knows to expect the unexpected and takes painstaking care to ensure questions are clear, concise, and applicable to all the respondents.

Similarly, there are several do's and don't's regarding the sequencing of the survey. Again, common sense often dictates many sequence decisions. For example, it is important to catch the respondent's interest right off the bat, so the lead questions should stimulate their interest. Questions relating to the same topic area should be grouped together, producing a certain logical organization to the survey. Within a given topic area, questions should flow from broad, general questions to more specific, not the reverse order. Personal or confidential questions should be placed at the end of the survey. By this time the respondent has answered all the other questions and a certain rapport has been developed in that the respondent is not less anxious about participating and is feeling more comfortable with the procedure. This is specifically critical for many church surveys which might be asking personal questions relating to an individual's spiritual or emotional need.

One final note regarding the questionnaire design is that the final survey should be as brief as possible, yet contain the necessary questions that will provide the information relating to the research objectives. Very few individuals have the time or patience to wade through a long survey containing a myriad of questions about numerous topics. The final survey is the result of an interactive process during which many questions are edited, taken out, moved, etc. No extraneous questions should remain. Each remaining question should have a specific purpose in providing the exact information deemed necessary by the researcher.

While the researcher can revise the survey numerous times, resulting in a concise, fine-tuned document, the final step in questionnaire design should be the use of a pretest. This involves actually administering the survey to a small group of respondents to detect any further ambiguity, bias, or structural problems with the design. Pretests are extremely helpful in that the respondents can often point out problem areas that the researcher was unaware of.

A similar critical element of more formal research is to develop an appropriate sampling plan. Like any other business conducting a survey, a church will need to make specific decisions regarding:

(1) **The sampling unit** — "Who is to be surveyed?" While the answer may seem obvious, it is not always the case. The researcher needs to clearly identify exactly who should be contacted. For example, is it any member in the household, or do we want only the father or mother? Are there any qualifiers involved — above a certain age, sex, member of the church, unchurched, or whatever? This area requires a specific description of who is to be surveyed as well as who is not wanted.

(2) **The sample size** — "How many people should be surveyed?" This decision will be based on tradeoffs. Certainly, we would all like large sample sizes responding to our survey. However, the more surveyed, the more time and money involved. Secondly, how large a sample size is also tied into how the data will be collected. Personal interviews take the greatest time and

moncy, as opposed to mail and telephone data collection, so this method may dictate smaller samples. Many people believe that if the research is worth anything it will require a large sample. Fortunately, this is not the case. Fairly reliable results can be obtained with relatively small sample sizes, provided certain sampling procedures are followed.

(3) **The sampling procedure** — "How should the people be chosen?" To begin with, the decision regarding the selected sampling procedure is based on the size of the target population to be surveyed. For example, if a church leader wants to survey the congregation for their input and the church is relatively small (less than 100), it would probably be feasible to conduct a census. This implies that the researcher attempts to survey every individual in the congregation. This doesn't imply every member responds. Some may refuse, others not around, etc., but the attempt to survey every individual was made.

On the other hand, if the congregation is relatively large, or perhaps a survey of residents in the surrounding community is wanted, then a census would be impractical due to time and cost considerations. In this situation the researcher must choose between a nonprobability sample or a probability sample. A nonprobability sample implies a subjective selection of respondents. In other words, those surveyed were selected by the researcher because they were convenient or were judged appropriate for whatever reason. For example, in conducting a congregational survey, a researcher may pick a particular Sunday to distribute the surveys to those who were in attendance that day. They were surveyed simply because they were there. The problem with nonprobability samples is that they are not truly representative of the target population and therefore cannot, or should not, be generalized. On the other hand, they are often quicker and easier than a probability sample.

A probability sample implies that every individual in the population had a known (generally equal) chance of being selected. Probability samples, therefore, are objective and unbiased. The sample selected or representative of the target population and the results can be generalized (within a certain margin of error). An example of a probability sample could be a large church with, say, 1000 members. The researcher, using a listing of these 1000 members, sends a survey to every 10th name on the list. The starting point is randomly selected (from 1-10) and then every tenth individual thereafter receives the survey.

There are several different types of both nonprobability and probability samples to choose from. A standard marketing research text can provide the details of these choices. The main decision for the researcher is if a census is not appropriate, whether to use a nonprobability type — for its ease and speediness, or a probability type which will produce a truly representative sample, allowing the use of standard statistical tests which will permit generalization to be made about the target population.

(4) **Means of contact** — "How should the subjects be contacted — telephone, mail, or personal interviews? Again, the researcher must choose among alternatives, each of which has its strengths and weaknesses.

In the past, personal interviews were the most common method of data collection, and market researchers believed the one-to-one personal contact was essential in gathering information. However, personal interviews are now the least common method, mainly due to the fact that it is by far the most expensive and time-consuming. Since the researcher can only deal with one respondent at a time, this method could be very unfeasible if a large sample size is desired. On the other hand, personal interviews are advantageous when the respondent will be asked to elaborate and/or detailed answers are desired. Similarly, if visual aids are utilized or something is being demonstrated, this would be the best method. Another important feature of personal interviews is that this method allows the respondent to provide feedback. This might be especially important for church-related surveys where the respondent is being asked some sensitive questions. By being reassured that the answers will be strictly confidential, this may enhance the willingness of the respondent to answer willingly and truthfully. Similarly, a personal interview allows the respondent to ask questions, seek clarification, and seek direction from the interviewer, features the other means of operation cannot provide.

In contrast, telephone interviews are now the primary means of collecting information. This is mainly due to their extreme efficiency in reaching a large number of people very quickly and also to being much less expensive than personal interviews. The interviewer's job is certainly much easier in that there is no wasted time traveling from one respondent to another. If one respondent on the list is unavailable, the interviewer can simply try the next person. Call-backs due to busy signals or someone not at home are also extremely efficient. The improvements in technology, such as computer-assisted telephone interviews or expansion of 800 numbers, have also enhanced the use of telephone interviewing. The main problem with telephone interviews is that the surveys should be very brief. While personal interviews allow the interviewer to probe and elicit detailed information from the respondent, telephone interviews must be very short or else respondents will either refuse to cooperate or hang up in the middle, wasting the entire effort.

Finally, mail surveys are also very efficient in that the researcher is able to reach large segments of the population. Compared to the other methods of collection, mail surveys are probably the least expensive. However, this can be very misleading since mail surveys, if done poorly, could result in very little return for the effort. Characteristically, the response rate for mail surveys is relatively dismal. A 25% response rate (1 out of 4 returned) is considered a relative benchmark. Most of us have received a mail survey at one time or another. If the topic is of no interest to us or it is too long or complex, then we probably tossed it right in the garbage. This is one reason why it is extremely critical to try to send mail surveys to those individuals we believe (or hope) have some interest in our topic. Similarly, the costs behind mail surveys are also more than one may think. For example, if we desire a decent response rate, it is essential to include a self-addressed stamped envelope. The researcher should try to make it as easy as possible to ensure the cooperation of the respondent. It is pretty bold to mail some stranger a survey, ask a variety of questions, some of them most likely sensitive or personal, and then expect them to provide their own envelope, stamp, and address it correctly so we get it back. One other drawback of mail surveys is that once they are mailed out, there is no turning back. If the survey contains questions that are confusing, or the directions are unclear, or other problems are present, then there is no chance to clarify these problems and we will most likely get a lot of strange responses back (if they respond at all). For those choosing mail surveys, it is extremely critical to perform a sufficient pretest to try to catch all the problems before we send then out.

However, one big advantage of mail surveys is that since there is no interviewer present and the respondent can complete the survey in complete privacy, respondents are more likely to provide confidential or sensitive information. A person will obviously feel much freer stating what they like and dislike about a church without a church elder waiting at their side for their completed survey.

The decision as to which method of collection is not an easy one. As stated, each has its strengths and weaknesses. Much depends on the type of survey being used, how long it is, how much detail is required, how large a sample size is required, the time and cost constraints involved, and who will be collecting the data. These are just some of the many issues to consider before determining the most appropriate method.

(5) **Data collection** — "Who will collect the data?" This issue is especially critical for churches. Can they use volunteers from the congregation or should they use professional interviewers? For example, if the church decides on personal interviews or telephone interviews to obtain information from people in the community, can they, or should they, attempt to train their members to perform the role of the interviewer? Again, there are no easy answers. The use of professional interviews or data collection services will greatly add to the cost of the project. On the other hand, can the church do a credible job in getting their own members to perform this task?

Data Analysis

The fourth step of the marketing research process is perhaps the most complicated to church leaders: making sense of the data that has been collected. Ideally, once the data has been collected, it needs to be put into a format that will answer the church's research questions. Again, most church leaders do not possess an expertise in statistics, so it is imperative that the researcher's purpose should not be to overwhelm the staff with number and highly sophisticated statistical techniques.

In examining a basic marketing research text, one can be overwhelmed by the section on data analysis in which numerous techniques, such as multivariate statistical analysis, regression analysis, analysis of variance, etc., are discussed. While there are many techniques available to analyze data, the researcher should only select those techniques that are appropriate for the type of data being collected. I have seen many of my marketing research students try to force-feed some of the more sophisticated statistical techniques on to data they've collected when very simple descriptive statistics (such as merely computing the average) would have been more appropriate and certainly more meaningful to the client.

Regardless of what techniques are utilized or what level of sophistication is required, the critical aspect of data analysis is to make the data more meaningful to the church leader so that they can use the information to satisfy the original research objectives and ultimately use this information to improve their decision-making capabilities.

Conclusions and Recommendations

Having analyzed the data, the final step of the research process should be to interpret the information and make specific recommendations. In research, many experts make a clear distinction between analysis and interpretation. When you analyze data, you state what the study found. Interpretation then goes beyond the statement of figures to tell why those figures are meaningful, or how they must be tied together to create a new vision of what is being studied. In essence, the researcher must look at the analysis of the information collected and ask, "What does this mean to the church?"

While many research reports focus too much on the technical aspects of their sampling plan or the sophisticated statistical techniques utilized to analyze the data, I believe the report should communicate the true findings in a manner meaningful and understandable to the church leader.

Ideally, in the final report, the interpretations should, in essence, bring the project full circle: recommendations, specific actions based on the information gathered that will enable the research objectives to be satisfied. This final step reiterates that the marketing research process is a logical, step-by-step of procedures that should enable the church leader to be more likely to offer findings that will enhance decision-making.

Implications for Churches Conducting Marketing Research

If a church desires to become more marketing-oriented, and more and more are moving in that manner, then they are committing themselves to try to identify and understand the needs and wants of the group of people they are currently serving and those they hope to attract and serve. Marketing research is the key tool to help churches first identify these needs and wants.

Unfortunately, many churches may tend to take their current members somewhat for granted. These individuals come to church, contribute their time and money, and participate in various church activities. However, it is extremely helpful to periodically obtain feedback from the congregation to see how well the church is meeting their needs and also perhaps to identify what particular needs are simply not being met. Surveying the congregation is a convenient way to find out members' likes and dislikes, desires, ideas, opinions, etc. Such information can be invaluable to determine how well the church is doing in meeting its members' needs and perhaps, equally important, to point out areas of need or opportunity on which the church should focus its future activities.

For those churches who wish to grow and are trying to attract part of the large segment of "unchurched" Americans, marketing research can again be a vital tool in trying to identify the issues and needs important to people in the community. Research in the community can point out if people are aware of the church, what, if any, image they have of it, or any basic impression they have of the church. In addition, church surveys could be used to help identify some of the underlying spiritual or emotional needs of community residents. This information might be helpful in guiding a church to perhaps establish certain services or outreach programs to help address these identified needs of the community.

Thus, whether a church is merely trying to keep its faithful members satisfied, or is desiring to attract the unchurched, it must first identify what these people need and want. Only then can they develop the appropriate offerings and services that will satisfy these personal needs and wants most effectively.

Endnotes

1. Philip Kotler and Alan R. Andreasen, *Strategic Marketing for Nonprofit Organizations,* Englewood Cliffs, NJ: Prentice-Hall, 1987, p. 202.

2. George Barna, *Marketing the Church,* Colorado Springs, CO: Navpress, 1988, p. 63-64.

3. William G. Zikmund, *Exploring Marketing Research,* Chicago, IL: The Dryden Press, 1991, p. 39-40.

4. George Barna, *Church Marketing,* Ventura CA. Regal Books, p. 57.

5. *Ibid.,* p. 61.

6. Zikmund, p. 123.

7. William Martin, "The Baptists Want You," *Texas Monthly,* February, 1977, p. 84.

5

Developing a Marketing Plan for Churches

Introduction

Successful marketing programs are usually based on an explicit marketing plan to guide the organization's action towards achievement of the desired objectives. Marketing planning has become a major activity in most firms. One survey found that over 90% of marketing executives were engaged in formal planning.[1] The executives, on average, spend 45 days a year involved in planning, and they rely most heavily on information from the sales force, management information systems, and internal marketing research. The developmental plans are an important function for marketing, one that is beneficial for improving both coordination and performance.

Planning incorporates the second half of the marketing concept definition discussed previously. A firm with a marketing orientation will first try to identify the needs and wants of its target market, which can often be accomplished through marketing research. The second half — developing programs to satisfy their target market's needs and wants — necessitates some type of planning activity: obtaining the needed information is a critical first step, but more importantly there must be mechanisms within the organization to utilize this information to design the strategies and tactics that will ultimately satisfy needs and wants more effectively than the competition. Planning provides that type of mechanism to accomplish the task.

Unfortunately, many churches have been very slow in incorporating planning into their scope of operation. Similar to many churches' reluctance to utilize any type of marketing research to identify the needs and wants of its constituents, there appears to be somewhat similar hesitancy to incorporate planning activities. While many pastors may spend a great deal of time "planning" their sermon, the scripture passages to be read, or the worship for a given week, they may not feel comfortable using the same basic planning concepts when it comes to marketing the church.

If a church leader believes in the benefits of a marketing orientation for the church, accepts the rationale for market segmentation, has identified the segment(s) the church hopes to attract, and understands the aid to decision-makers that marketing research can offer, then he/she most likely will be willing to investigate the components of planning and be willing to develop a marketing plan to help the church reach its potential. First and foremost, however, the church leader must be aware of the benefits of planning and understand how to develop a marketing plan most appropriate for meeting the needs of the existing members as well as attracting new people to the church.

Benefits of Planning

As mentioned previously, many churches do not develop formal marketing plans. Objections to planning might include the pastor's belief that they are too busy with day-to-day duties to have the time and/or resources to formulate a plan. Other church leaders may believe their church is too small to justify time spent on planning. (This is also a convenient reason why not to conduct any marketing research!) Others may claim that their church is unique and its uniqueness would not be served well by planning. To some church leaders, planning is equated to budgeting, and they perceive that by "budgeting" the church's resources they are, in essence, planning. Finally, as stated previously, the training that most pastors receive does not include any business-related topics so formalized planning may seem very foreign and intimidating to them.

In spite of these perceived obstacles, church leaders need to be aware of the very real benefits that finalized marketing plans can provide. To begin with, since most churches operate with constrained resources — financial, time, and personnel — planning can help church leaders better coordinate and allow the most effective utilization of these scarce resources. Churches cannot afford to waste time and money. Similarly, planning can help church leaders focus their efforts in the most efficient manner. It is likely churches will be faced with more problems and opportunities than they have the resources or capabilities to dedicate to them. Planning can aid churches in selecting those problems and/or opportunities that it can most effectively devote its limited resources to.

Since many church projects or programs will likely involve participation of church members, planning can be a great assistance in coordinating those activities when many individuals are involved. These days, many church members are likely pressed for time, and nothing would be more frustrating than being bogged down in some church-related activity that has no direction, no sense of completion, and utter confusion. Church leaders must realize that these members who are willing to donate their time and effort should be utilized in the most efficient manner so they can feel their effort is worthwhile and they can share in the joy of accomplishment. Planning would be especially critical in situations where many members are involved and it is essential certain activities are accomplished in the correct chronological order.

Another great benefit of planning with a church would be improved communication. A critical feature of formalized planning is feedback — basically, "How are we doing?" If a church has clearly defined goals and objectives, formalized planning can aid in communicating their accomplishment, in identifying what went wrong and recommending goal-specific corrective actions. Similarly, when members of the congregation are involved in a church project or program, planning can help by identifying the specific tasks needed to be accomplished, who is responsible for each action, as well as a proposed timetable for completion. Such information will be communicated to all the involved participants, which would provide a true sense of direction and camaraderie or team effect since all the involved members will be working toward the same goal.

Finally, a marketing plan for a church is very much like a road map. It identifies where we are right now and where we want to go. It provides the way(s) in which we want to get from here to there. It allows the church to keep track of the progress: how far have we gotten and how much farther do we have to go? Without any formalized planning, a church is like a driver with no end destination: merely driving with no direction, little awareness of time or energy wasted, no sense of completion, and no concept as to what has been accomplished or what needs to be accomplished.

Types of Planning

Planning from a marketing perspective can be thought of as two processes: (1) Strategic planning is the process of developing and maintaining a strategic fit between the organization's goals and resources and its changing marketing opportunities; (2) Marketing planning is the process of selecting target markets, choosing a strategic position, and developing an effective marketing mix to reach and serve the target groups and achieve organizational goals.[2]

In essence, strategic planning embodies the overall philosophy of the church, asking such broad-ranged questions such as: What kind of church are we? What kind of church do we want to be? These types of questions imply a long-term perspective in that it embodies the overall mission of the church. It also coerces church leaders to evaluate just where we are right now. Are we truly satisfying the spiritual and emotional needs of our members? Are we reaching out to the community and attracting others to become part of the church?

Strategic planning for churches is also analogous to the vision of the church leader. A pastor's vision for the church includes a feeling of where the church is, where we want to go, and how we're going to get there. Vision is much more than developing a mental picture of the past, present, and future. Vision is also the driving force behind the activity of a motivated leader or group of people. Vision should be viewed as the characteristic that is the responsibility of a leader and sets the leader apart from his/her followers. The leader has and communicates the vision; the followers accept and help carry out the vision.[3]

If a church leader possesses a vision for the church, it is essential that this vision is clearly communicated to the congregation. This vision must be clearly articulated so that the members can understand the mission of the church and how this vision will effect the shape of the church. More importantly, this vision must be accepted by the members. This could be a critical juncture for some churches. Some members may not understand the proposed vision or may simply not agree with it. Change, whether real or perceived, may be difficult for some church members to accept. However, if a church leader feels compelled to carry out the vision God has given him/her, then painstaking care must be taken to help those in doubt better understand the vision, its importance, and how it will help the church improve their ministries. If the members comprehend and believe in the vision, then the implementation of it will help bring it to fruition. If members feel a part of the vision, then they more likely will take an active role in making the vision a reality.

While strategic planning addresses the broad-ranging views of the church, marketing planning involves more of the nuts and bolts of planning. Rather than being philosophical or strategic planning, marketing planning offers specific actions and strategies and provides answers to more specific issues such as: What type of person(s) are we trying to attract? How can we most effectively reach this type of person(s)? What type of ministries and/or programs should we offer? How should we go about providing for those ministries and programs?

Strategic planning and marketing planning are closely interrelated for churches. While strategic planning focuses on the more macro issues of the church — broad goals that will allow the church to get to where it wants to be — marketing planning provides the specific strategies, tactics, and action plans that will enable the church to accomplish these goals. Thus, there is a very fine line between these two types of planning. One type logically leads to the second. The next section provides a marketing plan which incorporates both types of planning, and offers a logical step-by-step format appropriate for church leaders.

Suggested Marketing Plan Format for Churches

The suggested format involves a series of interrelated steps which flow from the very broad issues relating to strategic planning to the more specific issues covered by marketing planning. While all marketing textbooks provide some type of marketing plan, I have tried to design this one to be appropriate for churches and the unique environment in which they operate (Figure 5.1).

1. Mission of the Church
   • Who Are We?
   • Who Do We Want To Be?

2. Situational Analysis
   • Where Are We Now?
   • Evaluate the Internal Environment
   • Evaluate the External Environment

3. Planning Components
   • Identify Goals
     — What do we wish to accomplish?
   • Develop Specific Objectives
     — What specific outcomes do we want to
       achieve?
   • Determine Strategies
     — What specific courses of action should
       we pursue to satisfy our objectives?
     — What target market(s) should we pursue?
     — Develop appropriate marketing mixes to
       most effectively satisfy our target markets.
   • Develop Tactics
     — What specific hands-on activities should
       we utilize to put the strategies into action?

4. Marketing Control
   • Monitor performance to measure actual results
     against the plans and objectives.
   • Provide feedback to indicate where corrective
     action is needed.

Marketing Plan Format for Churches
Exhibit 5.1

Mission of the Church

To begin with, before any goals and objectives can be formulated, it is first necessary to be able to state the intended mission of the church. As mentioned previously, this involves what was referred to as strategic planning in asking such questions as: "What type of church are we?" and "What type of church do we want to be?" In essence the church is trying to discover a lot about themselves as well as their potential opportunities. The touchy part about developing the church mission statement is not to make it too narrow or too broad. It should be realistic, not a pie-in-the-sky'wish, and should hopefully be appealing and motivating to the congregation. Ultimately, the mission statement should provide a standard or benchmark against which every concept and approach can be tested to be certain that activities undertaken by the church are consistent with what the church is all about.

This first step is indeed critical for churches prior to devoting any attention towards goals, objectives, strategies, etc. In speaking with pastors of declining churches, George Barna found a common thread was their desire to do something for everybody. They had fallen into the strategic black hole of creating a ministry that looked great on paper, but had no ability to perform up to standards. Despite their worthy intentions, they tried to be helpful to everyone and they wound up being helpful to no one.

The stark reality is that every church has limited resources and has been called to accomplish a specific mission. Barna found in his research that successful churches resisted the impulse to be the answer to everyone's every problem by focusing their vision for ministry, by reaffirming their commitment to quality, and by recognizing their limitations. If they were to devote themselves to meeting every need in their marketplace, they would dissipate their resources and have no impact — the very tragedy that has befallen many Protestant churches in America.[4]

Situational Analysis

Having defined their purpose or reason as expressed in their mission statement, churches next need to evaluate their internal and external environment. This step is often referred to as "situational analysis," answering the question of "Where are we now?" Much of the information contained in a situational analysis should be factual data obtained by the church through its own internal records, secondly data sources, or any information gathered through the church's own marketing research. Easily obtainable factual information relating to the church's condition over the past several years, such as membership figures, budgets, worship service attendance figures, Sunday school evaluation, etc., might serve as a valuable input in describing the current internal environment of the church. Any collected information (marketing research) on the church community or the target market a church hopes to attract, including demographic characteristics, lifestyles, felt needs, attitudes, values, religious background, etc., would help the church leaders better understand how best to serve these constituencies.

Similarly, information gathered concerning the external environment of the church will aid the analysis of the ministry context. Such data might include the status of other churches in the community, their perceived target markets and goals, the proportion of unchurched adults in the community, the identification of key non-church (competitive) activities, etc.

All together, this variety of data and information should aid a church in merely assessing its current situation, its strengths and weaknesses, its potential threats and opportunities, and a realistic response to the question, "Where are we now?"

Planning Components

Having analyzed the current environment of their religious organization, church leaders should then try to develop four critical components of the actual planning efforts of the church. These elements include:

(1) identification of goals;

(2) development of specific objectives central to the goals;

(3) design of appropriate marketing strategies related to specific objectives;

(4) selection of specific tactics recommended for a particular strategy.

These steps should flow logically from one to another, and the progression of these steps infers movement from general concerns to more specific actions.

Goals

To begin with, the goals of a marketing plan represent the general outcomes church leaders wish to accomplish with their ministry. In identifying the goals of the church, one is answering the question, "What do we wish to accomplish?" Church marketing goals should provide the big picture, without getting bogged down in the details of measurement, style, approach, or anything else.[5] In addition, goals should be directly related to the church's mission statement and provide a sense of direction. Goals should be the manner in which church leaders answer the question, "Where do we want to go?"

While the goals being set should be somewhat broad, it is critical that the goals should also be challenging, but not set so high that they cannot be achieved. Unobtainable or totally unrealistic goals will damage the entire process, destroying the morale of those individuals participating in the planning process, and most likely result in the church refraining from doing any type of marketing planning in the near future. It is so important that the goals be achievable, resulting in a sense of accomplishment for the entire church, and providing definite positive reinforcement to the marketing planning process.

Finally, those churches that may consider attempting marketing planning will most likely identify more than one goal. It is important that the goals be placed in some order of priority to provide some focus to the process. Likewise, the number of goals should not be too large to render the process ineffective, and again, frustrating to those involved. A relatively small number of goals, all related to the church's mission statement, placed in order of importance, appears to be the most feasible goal-setting situation.

Objectives

While a church's goals may provide the big picture and a sense of direction, a marketing plan's objectives need to be more specific and concise. In addition, objectives should be measurable and achievable. As goals relate to the question, "What do we wish to accomplish?," objectives provide the answer to the question, "What specific outcomes do we hope to achieve?" Similarly, while objectives should be as specific as possible and measurable, inferring the results can be quantified. It is also important that they relate to a specific time period. This provides the frame in which these objectives should be accomplished and provides a guide for church leaders to plan to accomplish the desired outcomes by a certain date.

Just as goals should be relative to the mission statement of the church, objectives should be specifically related to one of the general goals of the church. Similarly, just as it was recommended that goals should be rated in order of their importance, so should objectives be ranked. Again, such a rank provides a clear-cut distinction as to what demands immediate attention and allows a chosen focus of the church's resources.

Strategies

While an objective should be a clear statement of exactly what outcomes a church wishes to achieve, a marketing strategy is the means by which the church accomplishes its objectives. In other words, the selected strategies should represent the specific causes of action the church will pursue to satisfy these objectives. Just as the objectives were tied directly to the goals of a church, the strategies should be tied directly to specific objectives. In addition, while marketing objectives are specific and measurable, marketing strategies are descriptive. They should describe how the quantifiable objectives will be met.

One essential dimension of marketing strategies is that they are dynamic in nature. For any given objective, there may be several potential strategies. Weinbert and Lovelock believe that in building a marketing plan, several different strategies usually must be constructed before the best one is chosen.[6] Indeed, for any church leader, to devise and evaluate various courses of action are two of the big benefits of an effective planning system. These alternative courses of action can then be weighed against the conclusions drawn from the situational analysis.

In developing specific strategies for a church, it will be most likely important to incorporate two specific components. First, if a church desires to grow and attract new members as one of its goals, it must clearly identify the target market it desires to pursue. A mass marketing — "shotgun" — approach is no longer feasible. The main advantages and implications of market segmentation were addressed in an earlier chapter. Many of today's growing churches that have adopted a marketing orientation to be more sensitive and responsive to its constituents' needs have also understood the importance and relevance of market segmentation. They have successfully segmented the market into distinct and meaningful groups and have chosen the appropriate segment(s) to pursue.

Having chosen the target market the church wishes to attract, the next step is to develop an appropriate marketing mix that will most effectively address the unique needs of the targeted segment. As mentioned previously, the marketing mix generally refers to the 4Ps of marketing, product, price, place and promotion, and represents the controllable variables that an organization uses to most effectively satisfy its intended market. Chapter 2 provides a translation of these controllable variables for churches. In designing marketing strategies, it is important that the resulting church marketing mix be designed so as to best appeal to the unique needs and wants of the target market. It is also imperative to realize that each segment of the population that a church wishes to attract would require its own unique marketing mix.

Tactics

The main intent in developing the marketing mix is to put forward the most effective means possible to achieve the marketing goals. Specifically, this implies developing an action program or set of tactics. These are the detailed, specific, hands-on activities that take place to put the strategy into action. Each marketing strategy needs to be turned into a specific set of actions for accomplishing the marketing objectives. Each strategy should be broken down into appropriate actions.

While strategies should describe what specific actions the church intends to pursue in order to accomplish its objectives, tactics should detail the specific activities to be utilized to put these strategies into action. In essence, tactics should clarify such issues as: Who will be involved and in which functions? Who has responsibility over the various aspects of the strategies? What resources will be utilized and how will they be allocated? Basically, the tactics recommended should provide the critical details required to successfully implement the marketing plan. These details, or the lack of such, will ultimately determine the success or failure of the church's objectives and goals.

Marketing Control

The final essential component of any marketing plan is the existence of some mechanism for ensuring the accomplishment of the short-term or long-term goals of the religious organization. Ultimately, some type of marketing control is necessary to maximize the probability that the organization achieves its goals and objectives.

To begin with, it is imperative that the church be able to monitor performance by measuring the ongoing results of a plan against the plan's goals and objectives. This implies that the marketing plan should include well-defined targets that are measurable and defined for a certain time period. Obviously, it is unrealistic to expect every objective to be accomplished, or within the specified time period. When deviations occur (and they will), the church's control mechanism should provide feedback to indicate where corrective action should be taken before it is too late.

The concept of monitoring performance on a weekly, monthly, or quarterly basis will allow church leaders to evaluate how strategies are working, which ones need to be changed, what alternative actions should be considered, and perhaps enable them to identify possible reasons when problems or deviations occur. It may require the church to readjust the predetermined objectives, or even the broadly defined goals, if deviations are significant.

With the existence of a marketing control mechanism to monitor performance and provide feedback on the church strategy's effectiveness, and to be able to identify just where certain programs are failing to achieve their objectives and perhaps the reason why, the marketing plan process is, in essence, a continual loop.

The marketing plan is a logical, step-by-step process, highlighted by the feedback provided by marketing control mechanisms that can call attention to minor deviations calling for contingency strategies to be utilized or development of new strategies to accomplish the predetermined objectives, or may even result in an adjustment of the original objectives and goals if deviations between what is expected and what actually happens is significant. Marketing control is somewhat like the glue that holds the whole process together.

Implications of Planning

While many churches have survived for many years without any type of formalized planning, the challenging and changing environment of churches will threaten many such churches in the next few years. These churches that wish to continue to prosper and grow during these difficult times will need to carefully determine their mission, knowing "who they are" and "where they want to go," and understand their environment, having identified their strengths and weaknesses, and being able to conceptualize "where they are now."

Such steps should lead a church to utilize its limited resources effectively and efficiently, and be able to develop a marketing plan to enable the mission of the church to be realized. While foreign to some church leaders, the components of a marketing plan should follow logically to one another and provide a sharper focus to accomplishing the vision of the ministry.

The benefits of marketing planning for churches were discussed earlier in the chapter. On the other hand, those churches that fail to plan in the turbulent times ahead may, unfortunately, be planning to fail. Perhaps this is an old adage, but it illustrates not only the importance of planning for churches, but also the severe ramifications for churches that do not adapt to the changes around and simply let nature take its course.

Endnotes

1. Christopher H. Lovelock and Charles B. Weinberg, *Public and Nonprofit Marketing,* Redwood City, CA, The Scientific Press, 1989, p. 5.

2. Shawchuck, Kotler, Wrenn and Rath, p. 212.

3. George Barna, *Marketing the Church,* Colorado Springs, CO: Navpress, 1988, p. 81.

4. Barna, *User Friendly Churches,* 1991, p. 51.

5. George Barna, *Church Marketing,* Ventura, CA: Regal Books, 1992, p. 168.

6. Lovelock and Weinberg, *op. cit.,* p. 109.

6

Product, Place, and Price Issues for Churches

Introduction

Any organization that is marketing-oriented is in essence following a two-step procedure. First, it is necessary to identify the needs and wants of the selected target market. This is the task of marketing research. Second, based on the gathered information concerning these needs and wants, the firm must develop the appropriate product/service that most effectively satisfies these needs and wants.

To best satisfy these identified needs and wants, marketers often utilize a marketing mix: the set of controllable variables that a firm combines and manipulates to make the "mix" as attractive to the target market as possible, while still adhering to the time and cost constraints of the organization. As mentioned previously, these controllable variables are often labelled the 4 P's of marketing. The *product* could include a tangible or intangible item and/or some combination of services. The *place* includes the where, when, and by whom the "product" is offered to the target market. *Promotion* implies any attempts to communicate to the target market about the "product" being offered. Finally, *price* is the cost to the intended market, either in terms of time or money.

This chapter will address the P's of product, place, and price, while the following chapter will discuss the wide range of promotional decisions facing a church.

Product

While the concept of the "product" is very clear for most organizations, in that they are offering a physical item for sale or providing an identifiable service, it is not as easy to define the "product" that a church is offering to its target market.

A church's product is obviously not something tangible that its constituents can pick out. A church is not trying to sell "Jesus" or sell the "Bible" or sell "salvation." Instead, a church is offering its target market a potpourri of different program offerings that might include the actual worship service, Bible classes, Sunday school classes, available counseling, outreach programs, etc. The variety of such offerings will vary from church to church, but such components represent a variety of different "products" that the church is providing to most effectively address the spiritual and emotional needs of its members and/or target market it hopes to attract.

Similar to the actual offerings of church, an equally important component of a church's "product" is the offering of potential relationships. First, the church is encouraging its members to develop a deep and fulfilling relationship with Jesus Christ. The worship, preaching, counseling, classes, and activities offered within a church aid one's personal relationship with God. On the other hand, the church is also offering potentially meaningful relationships with others. Helping one to feel connected with others, enjoy a sense of belonging or a sense of community, and the chance to develop solid friendships with others is another important component of a church's product. It is estimated that many Americans are extremely lonely, and the church offers a possible solution to the aloneness many seek to escape. Similarly, with such a mobile society, many feel themselves with no family or friends nearby and again, the church may represent an extended family to such individuals.

Thus, it is evident that it is extremely difficult to define specifically a church's product. Not only are some components tangible and others intangible, but they will be perceived differently and valued differently by the members of the congregation. Similarly, some aspects of the church's product will be welcome by some as a means of addressing their own spiritual and emotional needs, while others will *not* be receptive to the same components. A church cannot be all things to all people. All churches operate under time, cost, and staffing constraints.

Recognizing their limited resources, church leaders need to determine what components of the church "product" they should focus on to most effectively address the needs of their intended constituents. George Barna discovered that successful churches resisted the impulse to be the answer to everyone's every problem by focusing on their vision/ministry, by reaffirming their commitment to quality, and by recognizing their limitations. If they were to devote themselves to meeting every need in the marketplace, they would dissipate their resources and have no impact — the very tragedy that has befallen the majority of Protestant churches in America.[1]

Regardless of which components or how many components of a church's product are emphasized, it is critical that those selected components have value in the members' eyes and provide satisfaction of their needs. The ultimate value of a product should be based on its abilities to satisfy the members' spiritual and emotional needs, not because it is a "favored" offering of the church leader. Many churches have good intentions, but their efforts are ill-placed. Many churches emphasize making their programs work, which either means having a certain number of people involved, or viewing the program as an end in itself, rather than a means to an end. The focus of a church's product should be on satisfying the spiritual and personal needs of the *people*, not on the development and numerical success of the *program* being offered.[2]

To help the church leaders better identify the components of their own church's "product," the following list of questions is provided. The list is by no means inclusive, but tries to incorporate some of the key determinants of the overall church product. To facilitate the use of these questions, bipolar attributes are provided for each question.

Based on the identified spiritual and emotional needs of our members and/or the targeted group we hope to attract:

- What should be the style of worship?
  (Traditional, Structured vs. Contemporary, Flexible)
- What type of music should be used within the worship style?
  (Traditional, Old Hymns vs. Modern, Upbeat Praise Songs)
- What should be the focus of the sermon?
  (Strict interpretation of the Bible vs. Teaching to develop one's relationship with God)

- What should be the focus of the church?
  (Concerned primarily with the needs of its own members vs. Spreading the news of the Gospel to as many as possible)
- What is our spiritual perspective?
  (Emphasis on the Bible vs. Active in the social issues of the day)

The next set of questions is provided for church leaders to assess the feasibility of other offerings based on the needs and wants of their desired publics.

- Should we provide some type of Adult Bible Classes?
- Should we commit our resources to building an active children and youth ministry? How much emphasis should we put on developing child care, Sunday School classes, Youth Groups, and youth-related activities?
- Should we help set up small, home groups to help encourage our members to develop meaningful relationships with one another and also help one another grow in their own personal relationship with God?
- Should we offer counseling programs to help those with problems (marital, substance abuse, stress, family life, etc.)?
- Should we sponsor sports teams for our members and others to participate (softball, basketball, coed volleyball, bowling, etc.)?
- Should we be active in addressing pressing needs in the community by providing appropriate outreach programs?
- Should we offer regular social activities for our members and those in the community we wish to attract?

Place

In the secular world, "place" decisions refer to where the product/service is made available to its target customers. If the product is not at the right place at the right time, then potential customers cannot purchase the item. As stated previously, churches offer a variety of products to their constituents. Decisions must be made as to how best to make these "products/services" available to their members or desired publics.

For most consumer products, customers visit retail stores to choose the items they desire, pay for them, and take them home. Church "place" activities are somewhat more complex in that some of the church's products are made available within the church building, while other products offered will be available outside the boundaries of the church facility. Just as the dimensions of the church "product" are complex, so too are the dimensions of "place" concerns.

Church Facilities

It is obvious that some of the church's products will be made available on the church grounds. Some aspects of the church's product, such as worship, preaching, Sunday School classes, counseling, and social interaction, take place within the church's facilities. It is important that the members feel comfortable within the church facilities and, as a result, this should aid the satisfaction of the services they attend in the building.

While some churches may be in a position to build a new facility, the vast majority of churches are currently set in a given location, and therefore must make the most of their existing facilities. As a result, this section will *not* address the complex issue of buying land, designing new structures, etc. Instead, key concerns regarding the existing facilities of a church will be addressed.

One aspect of a church's existing facility that cannot be changed is its location. Most likely, the church is conveniently located for most of its current members. Church growth specialists indicate that people generally will not travel more than six miles to get to a church.[3] This is an important consideration when church leaders are trying to determine what segments of the community they may be trying to attract. Geographic segmentation appears to be a very real concern for identifying potential target markets.

Many people who wind up choosing a church 15 or 20 miles from home find out that one of two things happens. Some learn (the hard way) that the commute is so long it discourages them from coming back for other church activities; they unintentionally become "Sunday morning members." Other people, not content to limit their involvement to Sunday morning, decide that maybe the church was not the ideal church after all, and reinitiate their church search.

This time, they specifically look for a congregation that is within a short drive from home.[4]

Another concern regarding a church's facility is its size. When the main worship hall becomes overcrowded, this may result in some negative ramifications. Nobody likes to be stuck outside the main room, either standing or on folding chairs. Such overcrowding makes it stressful for members (finding a seat), probably discourages newcomers or visitors from attending again, and inhibits the service from being a meaningful experience. If such overcrowding persists, church leaders need to consider alternatives, such as adding another service, or even expansion of the existing facilities.

If a church desires to grow, it is important to recognize the 80% rule of thumb that many growth specialists have discovered. This rule of thumb implies that once a church reaches 80% capacity for its service, it will be unable to further attract new members. Such a condition similarly implies the necessity of additional services or expansion.

When churches grow and begin to stretch the capacity of their worship service, decisions need to be made as to how many worship services to offer its constituents. Perhaps one service a week on Sunday mornings is no longer feasible due to an overcrowding situation. If more than one service is planned, then at what times should they be offered? Some churches have found a nice balance for their members by offering an early Sunday morning and late Sunday morning service. Other churches have found that Sunday night service is a viable and preferred option for its members.

Regardless of what day(s) of the week, what hour of the day, or how many worship services are offered, the important consideration is that the level of service provided is compatible with the size of the congregation. Similarly, these decisions should be made with the time constraints or needs of its members in mind so that the services offered are convenient and compatible with the assumed hectic schedules of its members.

A similar concern regarding size is the availability of convenient parking. Again, an overcrowding in the church parking facility may similarly result in a stressful situation for some, having to park in the street far from the church, etc., and may also result in a newcomer's decision not to come back. Just as overcrowding in the worship service is a serious concern and must be dealt with, so too are problems of inadequate parking. If church leaders want their constituents to have a meaningful worship experience, they need to ensure that those people are not stressed-out, exhausted, and frustrated by long, enduring experiences in the parking lot.

Another key issue for church leaders is the appearance of the facility. The facilities of a church represent an initial image to newcomers. If the facilities have not been maintained, and there is a great deal of dilapidation, such an image could portray a very negative message to those visiting that this is a church in decline and not a source of a vibrant ministry.

Understandably, many small churches are subject to severe budget constraints and may not be able to properly handle all needed improvements. However, it is essential for church leaders to do what they can to present a clean, comfortable, and warm environment that makes its members feel "at home" and also may make visitors feel welcome.

Of similar concern is the condition of the nursery or child-care facilities. This is a vital consideration for families, and especially if the church is trying to attract people in the community. Parents today demand quality child care. The nursery should be clean and uncluttered. Doug Murren advises churches that hope to attract baby boomers with children to plan the children's facilities so that they are "visitor-friendly." He advises to make it easy for visiting families to find where to take their children. Nothing is more disturbing to a visiting parent than having to wander confused around an unfamiliar church, looking for the place where the children are to worship. He also advises to design child-care facilities that emphasize and appeal to children. Show by all that you do with your buildings and grounds that kids are a priority in your church. Then ensure that those facilities are always clean.[5]

Beyond the Church

Of equal concern regarding a church's place decision is the availability of various products/services outside the geographical boundaries of the church facilities. Some people may perceive a church as being limited to whatever takes place on the church grounds. However, by equating "place" with the physical location of the church, this results in a very narrow-minded perspective to what the variable truly entails.

In the secular world, the "place" variable also implies the distribution of a product from point of production to the point of consumption. In a similar light, an analogous perspective for church marketing would be to examine how a church "distributes" its product offerings to its desired constituents. This viewpoint moves beyond the physical boundaries of a church and allows a church to focus on "how" it goes about satisfying the needs and wants of its desired publics.

As mentioned previously, one of the key components of a church's product is the offering of potential relationships with others. In today's hectic, mobile society, many are longing for a sense of belonging, true meaningful friendships, and the opportunity to interact with others who share common interests. Many successful churches have moved beyond the boundaries of the churchgrounds by encouraging a sense of intimacy among members by breaking the church into smaller units, such as home Bible study groups or kinship groups where small groups of members meet regularly at someone's home, worship together, support and encourage each other, and help one another foster a deeper, more meaningful relationship with God.

By obtaining a sense of intimacy and friendship with others through such small groups, individuals are likely to feel connected with the church overall and will likely be more active participants in church activities. The sense of connectedness and belonging achieved through these groups can be of great benefit not only to the individual but also to the vitality of the church's ministry.

In addition, many churches may find it feasible to sponsor certain activities such as softball teams, coed volleyball, picnics, social events, youth groups, singles' clubs, etc. Such activities provide an opportunity for the involvement of its members and another chance to interact with other members. The sense of camaraderie, participation, and pure enjoyment will further strengthen one's commitment to a church and a sense of belonging.

These church-sponsored activities and small groups that are placed outside of the church's facilities are so important in that they are often more directly involved in addressing the individual needs and wants of each church member. Whenever meaningful relationships are being forged, individuals encouraged or supported, and aided in the development of their own relationship with God, this represents the actual "place" of church marketing.

Price

In the secular world, the "price" stands for the amount of money a customer must pay to receive the product or service. It generally implies some type of monetary compensation. However, the "price" variable of church marketing is somewhat more complex. Just as identifying the actual product being offered by a church is complicated, determining the "price" for a member or potential newcomer is difficult to define.

Certainly, part of the implied "price" of a church member is the financial support provided. Churches depend on the financial support of its members and could not survive without it. There have been scores of books written on stewardship or how to increase members' givings, so this section will not try to follow that path. Instead, this section discusses the concept of giving in regards to the marketing-oriented church.

Prior to his founding of Willow Creek Community Church, Bill Hybels took a door-to-door survey in the Chicago area. One topic he asked of those who didn't actively attend a local church is "Why not?" One common theme was that "Churches are always asking for money." Today, with his services attracting 15,000 or more people, newcomers or visitors are informed that the church doesn't want their money until they've decided they want the church.[6]

Similarly, George Barna asks, "Think about what a traditional church is like. An old person greets you at the door and hands you a mimeographed bulletin. You sit in an uncomfortable pew and stare at the back of someone's head. You sing 400-year-old songs and listen to a 20-minute talk about theology. Then they ask you for *money* and kick you out."[7]

The point of these two illustrations is that many people are troubled by a church's pleading for support without getting anything comparable in return. Just as in the secular world, consumers balance the expected benefits against the expected costs. If an individual feels isolated in a church, does not feel he/she is growing, and perceives no real or intangible benefits from the church's product, then that person will most likely be reluctant to pledge support to the church, either financial or in terms of a true commitment.

As stated previously, churches must offer the types of offerings that best satisfy the identified spiritual and emotional needs of their publics. If the church's product does not address these needs, then it will be very difficult to motivate these individuals to contribute their time and money to the church.

On the other hand, if an individual is growing in his/her relationship with God, is developing meaningful relationships with other church members, and is experiencing a sense of belonging, then this person will be more apt to willingly contribute to support the church and its ministry. Lyle Schaller believes that a church will reap in results what it sows in expectations. He suggests, "As members enrich their lives by working for the church, the payoff to the church in mundane things like cash is almost a matter of course."[8]

In addition to members' financial support, churches also depend on their members' commitment of time, energy, support, and participation in the various activities that ultimately help the church to thrive and prosper.

Unlike most organizations, churches rely heavily on volunteers. Churches are constantly faced with a shortage of people to provide the types of programs and services that reflect the church's ministries. Even the smallest churches need volunteers to teach Sunday school, sing in the choir, help in the maintenance of the facilities, and serve on committees.

Whether an individual willingly participates in these activities and donates their time and effort is analogous to whether or not they will willingly provide financial support to the church. In today's hectic pace, it is always possible for an individual to justify why he/she can't participate or serve on committees, etc. If the person feels his/her spiritual and emotional needs are *not* being met by the church, this person can easily find convenient excuses not to participate.

On the other hand, if an individual perceives these needs are being met by the church, then he/she will be more willing to help in some manner in church-related activities, as well as being more willing to contribute financially. George Barna found that in successful "user-friendly" churches, there seemed to be an ample supply of qualified and capable people who were willing to donate their most precious resources — time and ability — for the benefit of the church.[9]

Implications

A marketing-oriented church, having identified the spiritual and emotional needs of its members and/or the target group it hopes to attract, must then develop an appropriate marketing mix to most effectively satisfy those needs and wants.

The marketing mix represents the controllable variables of an organization and is comprised of what is commonly referred to as the 4 P's — product, place, price, and promotion. The variables are manipulated until the resulting mix is most appropriate for the desired publics.

Unlike the secular world, where the variables of product, place, and price are more easily defined, these variables for church markets are indeed more complicated. While the church is not actually "selling" a physical item, its product is comprised of many different components, some tangible and others intangible.

Of similar concern to church leaders is how to best distribute these various product offerings. While some aspects of a church's product may be available at the church's facilities, other critical components are obtained by its constituents outside of the church's physical boundaries.

Finally, once a church has developed its product offerings and determined how best to make them available to its constituents, then the intended individuals must evaluate whether the potential benefits and availability of the church's offerings balance the perceived price or costs. If the church has successfully provided the types of programs and offerings that address the spiritual and emotional needs of the individual and made them obtainable either within church facilities or outside of the church, then that person is more likely to be a willing participant and contributor, not only financially, but also in his/her time, effort, abilities and support of church-related functions.

The key point is that church leaders view the 4 P's as interrelated variables, not as independent, isolated issues. These controlled variables are tied together in that they represent the total package the church is offering its desired public. Decision in one of the variables should be evaluated in terms of its effect on the others. While this chapter illustrated the interrelationship of product, place, and price of marketing, the next chapter discusses promotional decisions affecting churches — i.e., how to most effectively communicate to the church's desired publics about the ministries and offerings.

Endnotes

1. George Barna, *User Friendly Churches,* Ventura, CA: Regal Books, 1991, p. 51.
2. George Barna, *Finding a Church You Can Call Home,* Ventura, CA: Regal Books, 1992, p. 86.
3. George Barna, *Church Marketing,* Ventura CA: Regal Books, 1992, p. 122.
4. *Ibid.,* p. 123.
5. Doug Murren, *The Baby Boomerang,* Regal Books, Ventura, CA, 1996, p. 116.
6. Thomas A. Stewart, "Turning Around the Lord's Business," *Fortune,* September 25, 1989, p. 119-120.
7. Brad Edmondson, "Bringing in the Sheaves," *American Demographics,* August 1988, p. 32.
8. Stewart, *op. cit.,* p. 120.
9. Barna, *User Friendly,* p. 162.

7

Promotional Decisions for Churches

Introduction

Promotion is often the most intrusive element of a firm's marketing mix, and often the most misunderstood. As stated previously, many people perceive marketing to be primarily advertising since one cannot escape its presence. Many believe advertising is deceptive, encourages senseless materialism and generally lowers the general level of taste. On a smaller scale, many people as a result equate the term promotion also with advertising for many of the same reasons. However, promotion incorporates several other important functions aside from advertising that an organization can use to communicate to its target market. These other functions include publicity, personal selling, sales promotion, which might involve contests, demonstrations, or exhibits, and direct marketing. The point is the marketer has a variety of methods that can be utilized to reach the desired constituencies. The collection of these methods is often referred to as an organization's promotion mix.

Perhaps a more realistic way to define promotion is as a means of communication. Basically, promotion implies communication about the product or service that is being offered. Similarly, a marketing-oriented church that has identified the types of programs and ministries it plans to offer and has also identified the target market(s) it wants to reach must determine the best way to communicate these offerings to its desired public. A church may have developed top-notch programs, and these programs may truly be well received by the type of person it hopes to attract. However, unless there is an effective means of communication, the intended target market will remain unaware of the church's ministries, the time and effort spent designing the church's programs will be wasted, the church's attempt to grow and reach out to the community will stagnate, damaging the morale of those involved, and the well-intended goals of the church will never be reached. In essence, promotion is the "glue" of an organization's marketing mix — holding together the other controllable variables.

While poor promotion can ruin an otherwise well-defined marketing plan, it is also critical that a church make sure it can deliver what it promises. An old marketing axiom says that the fastest way to kill a poor product is to advertise it heavily.[1] It may be more damaging to the credibility or reputation of a church if it continually promotes messages or promises to its intended target market which it cannot deliver. If a church adopts a motto such as "We care about you" and successfully communicates this message to the public, nothing will be more damaging than a newcomer coming to church and being ignored by all the regular members. Many churches these days tend to utilize similar catchphrases using words like friendly, caring, loving, etc. Those that promote such characteristics must make sure they can deliver these promises, otherwise that image can be shattered very quickly and that person will most likely never return.

Another key consideration regarding effective communication is that the church has clearly identified the segment of the population they are trying to reach. Again, this goes back to the importance and benefits of market segmentation discussed earlier. However, a church, having selected a particular segment, must pick the appropriate means of promotion to most effectively reach them. Promotional strategies for reaching unchurched baby-busters may be very different than those for reaching older baby-boomers.

Obviously, communication is a very complex and demanding process. Ultimately, it demands that the church has clearly identified the programs and ministries it wants to offer, selected the segment of the community that it wishes to attract and whose spiritual needs will be most effectively satisfied by the church's ministries, and finally selected those promotional elements that will allow it to most effectively communicate these offerings to the intended publics. Ineffective communication will prevent churches from growing and will doom even the most elaborate and detailed marketing plan.

If churches want to maximize their potential, it is essential they understand the communication process.

Communication Process Model

Since promotion can be defined as a means of communication, it is helpful to first understand the basic communication process. While there are several models of communication, the one utilized here is fairly simplistic, yet incorporates the primary elements of the communication process.

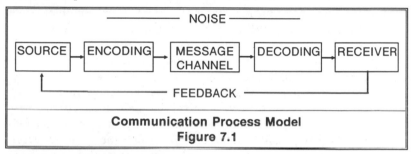

Communication Process Model
Figure 7.1

This communication process model offered here basically involves a source attempting to transmit or communicate a message to a receiver. In church marketing, the source is obviously the church, while the receiver is the desired constituent (church member, member of target market, unchurched, etc.). The other three components are critical functions of the communication process.

Encoding refers to the source trying to translate its message into symbolic form that it hopes will be noticed and well received by the receiver. For example, a church may know that roughly 60% of the community is unchurched, and they view their target market as the unchurched baby boomers. Their goal is to entice some of these unchurched baby boomers to come visit and become aware of their programs and ministries. This may certainly be a worthy and challenging goal. The problem is: how should a church convey the message about what the church is and what they are offering to a target population that is likely uninterested and perhaps unmotivated to attend? The difficult task of encoding is to translate the church's message symbolically in such a way that will catch the unchurched baby boomer's attention, make them at least aware of the church and its offerings, and hopefully stimulate some interest into possibly

visiting the church. Should a church use words, illustrations, testi-
monies, a catchy slogan, creative design, sponsored events, or whatever to best convey their message?

The message channel involves the method or vehicle through
which the message will be transmitted. While encoding involved
the translation of the selected message, the message channel involves the actual channels through which the message moves from
the source to the receiver. Such channels may involve use of various media sources, such as paid advertising, spots on television,
radio, newspapers, billboards, etc. It may involve face-to-face interaction, basically word-of-mouth which is an extremely effective
means of communication for churches. Or it might involve obtaining publicity for the church from various sources. Since most
churches operate with limited funds for promotion, they must be
very careful allocating where these scarce resources should be utilized. Similarly, church leaders must try to understand the most appropriate channels to reach their intended target market to make
sure that their message is being received by their intended receiver.

While encoding involves the source's translation of the message, decoding is actually the process by which the receiver assigns
meaning to the symbolic message. In essence, decoding is the translation by the receiver of the message that is being sent. While the
process of decoding is obviously personal and will vary from person
to person, churches should try to put themselves in the "shoes of the
receiver." If they are trying to reach unchurched baby boomers,
how do they think this type of person will react to their catchy slogan on a billboard, or their advertisement in the newspaper, or perhaps a call or letter from a church member? How will the
unchurched baby boomer interpret these messages and what, if any,
impact will it have on their attitude toward the churches or their
behavior regarding church visitation? Again, this function could
render the intended communication goal ineffective if the person is
turned off by the message, finds it totally inappropriate, or remains
completely indifferent.

The critical feature of this communication process model is
that there is some feedback to direct the entire process. Feedback
implies that the message was received and understood by the receiver and produced some type of response. For example, a church
implementing a promotional campaign to attract unchurched baby
boomers must realize that their message will not be reached by all
of the intended segment, nor will it produce any type of response

from most of this group. Yet, the promotional program might be viewed with success if the church received several inquiries from the group, or noticed several new people visiting the church shortly after the campaign. Other feedback may be even more subtle. For example, church members may hear from friends or relatives that they noticed the church's message on the "fill in the blank" (TV, radio, newspaper, billboard, outreach program, etc.). While these people who communicated may not wish to visit the church, their communications at least imply that the church's message was received and at least made some of this segment aware of the church and its ministries.

The first element of the communication process model is noise in the system. Noise is a "catch-all" term which includes any interference that inhibits the effectiveness of communication. This could imply the intended receiver was busy or occupied during the transmission of the message, the existence of competing messages, inappropriate media selection, or even poor message planning. Whatever the source, noise will hinder the communication process and prevent the message from reaching the receiver in the manner in which it was intended.

Types of Communication

As stated earlier, the success or failure of any marketing plan will ultimately be determined by how effectively a church can communicate its message to its intended target market. Any church is generally faced with two different constituencies that it must effectively communicate with. First, a church must continue to keep its current members informed and aware of the church's activities and programs. No church can afford to have its members become disillusioned, uninformed, and eventually inactive. Secondly, most churches need some level of growth and, therefore, desire to attract new members. Again, this implies a church has a vision for its ministries and has carefully identified the segment of the population that it believes can most effectively satisfy their spiritual needs with its planned programs and ministries.

As a result, George Barna stated there are two basic types of communication necessary to market a church's ministry (Figure 7.2).[2] He refers to the type of communication the church uses to deal with the people who are already members as "retention commu-

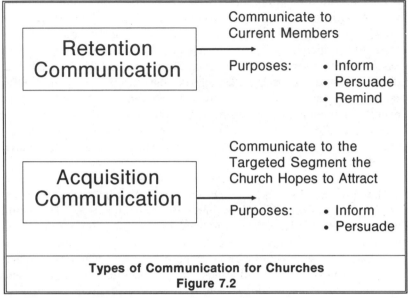

Types of Communication for Churches
Figure 7.2

nication." In essence, the goal of this type of communication is to describe church news and make the members aware of the opportunities and experiences the church is offering. In order to retain its current members, communication is important to give them direction, insight, and motivation for their active engagement in their faith. The point of retention communication is to ensure that the regular members feel involved and part of the church family. Whether they actually participate in the church program or activity may be secondary to the point that they were made aware of the offering and it now becomes their decision whether or not to attend. I have seen situations where some church members were visibly annoyed when they learned after the fact that a new Bible class had started, or a church picnic was held, or whatever, and they were not informed of these activities. The lack of communication may lead to an uneasy feeling among some members and may lead them to further distance themselves from church-related activities.

Marketing generally defines the three main objectives of promotion to be (1) informing, (2) persuading, and (3) reminding. Retention communication can often incorporate all three of these objectives. Members need to be informed of the church's plans, goals, and activities, and afterwards persuaded to attend and participate. Messages of this type should contain the basic factual information for the member to process — in essence, informing them of the needed facts. Similarly, the message could also include some persuasive attempts on the part of the church to encourage attendance or participation (perhaps providing time and/or resources). Obviously, reinforcement of the message is always helpful, so follow-up messages can greatly remind members of the activities and reiterate the key details.

On the other hand, in order to grow or even survive, churches today must continually enlist new members in the church and encourage their active involvement in church programs. While retention communication is vital to hopefully retain members, Barna cautions churches from focusing solely on retention messages. He believes such congregations tend to become ingrown and experience numerical stagnation and limited community influence. As a result, he advises churches to deploy what he refers to as "acquisition communication" as one of their overall promotional objectives.

Acquisition communication is more complex because it involves more uncertainty. Retention communication is aimed at church members, whose background and spiritual needs should be somewhat understood by church leaders, and is in essence a captive audience, easily reached and accessible. In contrast, acquisition communication is focused on the segment of the population the church hopes to attract. The spiritual and emotional needs of the intended target market are not so easily defined (marketing research can help) and it will certainly be much more difficult reaching this group effectively with the church's intended message.

Regarding the three objectives of promotion, acquisition communication initially must focus on informing as its main thrust. Its target market must, in essence, be made aware of the church, its programs and ministries, and the message the church wishes to transmit. Ultimately, the church must make these individuals aware of the intended image of the church (or the image it hopes to convey). Many people in the community may not even know the church exists or what makes it different from other churches in the community. Initially, this type of communication must overcome these individuals' lack of awareness about the church and provide the basic factual information regarding church activities that they can process.

While the factual information about the church (where, when, what) must be provided, there should also be attempts to provide some persuasion in the message. Ideally, acquisition communication should also overcome the individual's inertia by using persuasion to create a favorable psychological attitude that will ultimately get the person to take action and visit the church or attend one of its programs or activities. While there are a lot of unchurched Americans, there is also a great deal of competition among churches trying to reach them. A marketing-oriented church must attempt to use persuasion in their message in an attempt to differentiate themselves from others and appear to be more effectively addressing the spiritual needs and wants of the desired target market.

The difficult task for churches is to develop both types of communication. It is a difficult balancing act since those churches that are overly focused on retention communication will find it difficult to grow and attract new members and also be a viable force in the community. Similarly, those churches that overemphasize acquisition communication run the risk of alienating and possibly losing their current members who may feel their spiritual needs are being neglected at the expense of constantly trying to reach out for new members. While difficult, church leaders must try to find the right balance between these two diverse but equally important types of communication.

Inappropriate Promotional Strategies for Churches

Obviously, one of the key determining factors for the success of a church's marketing efforts is its ability to effectively communicate information to its target audience. The important issue for most churches is that having identified the target market(s) they hope to reach and having determined the scope and objective of the message, how does the church deliver the message effectively, while obviously subject to severe cost constraints? Most churches do not have the luxury of a large advertising budget to hire a creative team, have a professional message created, and buy a series of spots during prime-time television shows. Their budgets for promotional strategies will most likely be limited. They may have to solicit volunteers from the congregation who perhaps have a marketing or advertising background to help formulate the promotional strategies. These cost and staffing constraints necessitate that the churches do not exhaust their limited resources by engaging in inappropriate and ineffective promotional strategies.

For example, George Barna describes a newspaper ad for a church that was hoping to reach the unchurched. The ad, while appearing very professional and eye-catching, featured a very stern, almost angry pastor, seated in a chair with a Bible in his hand, who stared straight into the camera. The large, bold caption above the picture read: "Come hear Pastor X preach on why most people are going straight to hell."[3]

The church failed to recognize that their communication entered a dimension in which emotion runs deep. Many readers of the ad, however, would interpret the message as a guilt-producing one that placed the church and its people in a holier-than-thou light and characterized the reader as lost and hopeless. Not great motivation to climb out of bed Sunday morning to hear an angry-looking person rail against damnation.[4]

The point is that in trying to inform the unchurched and trying to persuade them to attend a local church, fear tactics or attempts to produce shame or guilt are likely to fail. Churches face intense competition today from many sectors: secular activities (movies, sport, travel), religious organizations (local congregations, TV ministries, Eastern religions) and human potential offerings (humanism, New Age, etc.). With such intense and diverse competition, churches should not try to communicate their message and ministries through guilt-producing techniques.

Similarly, many churches' main method of promotion is a newspaper ad which appears on Saturday on the religion page along with all the other church ads. Many of these ads are purely factual — providing the basic information of where and when, the name of the pastor, etc. There is generally very little in these ads that could possibly persuade an unchurched individual to attend or even differentiate one church from all the others. I seriously doubt how effective these ads could be. First, they are all lumped together — a mass of small-sized ads for different churches, all providing the same basic information. Secondly, who reads the religion page? Most likely people who already belong to a church and/or have an interest in the religious activities in their community. Perhaps more importantly, how many unchurched Americans spend their time scouring the religion page?

In contrast, I was intrigued by an ad by a church in my community that appeared not in the religion page, but right smack in the middle of the sports section — the only one of its kind. While it provided the necessary factual information, it also listed all the various programs of its ministry — which were quite extensive. It includes singles' groups, support groups for the divorced, youth groups, family activities, social activities, other support groups, etc., — something for everyone. The fact that it provided additional information that might persuade an individual to attend and the fact it appeared in, of all places, the sports section(!!) was very unique and totally different from all the other church newspaper ads. Not surprisingly, this church started a few years ago, is the fastest-growing church in the area and has become one of the largest in all of Central New York.

As stated previously, some churches have adopted clever, catchy phrases as their motto or slogan. Again, the problem is that the church better be able to deliver what it promises or else all credibility will be lost and the motto may result in more harm than good. The church needs to ask itself whether or not it can deliver what the message promises. In the secular world, not delivering what is promised would be labeled "deceptive advertising." Obviously, churches, while having good intentions in their promotional offerings, can also be guilty of this.

For example, George Barna describes such a situation involving a small church in the Midwest. This particular church strongly promoted its motto, which was "the friendliest church in town." Certainly, the motto was a nice, nonoffensive expression, but the church's reliance on the motto in their promotional strategies developed some unanticipated negative ramifications. First, the motto effectively alienated the church from others in the community. Second, the church failed to realize any growth, despite a healthy number of visitors passing through the doors. The fact was the message promised something the congregation did not delivery.[5]

Another problem is that some churches, while obviously subject to budget constraints regarding promotional activities, may select a medium solely based on its low, low rate. While it is certainly prudent to be cost-conscious, it is also important to evaluate just what you're getting for your money. Each week I received a "Pennysaver" newspaper which includes hundreds of small ads, most of which describe items for sale, upcoming garage sales, services offered — such as lawnmowing, painting, handyman jobs, etc. Interspersed among these types of ads are also ads for various churches. Again, they provide only factual information, but I wonder how effective they are in attracting new people. The advantage of these ads is that they are relatively inexpensive and are mailed to people in the community, but I am suspect of their impact.

Similarly, others caution against choosing a medium based on its low rate rather than on its cost per 1000 readers/listeners, or viewers. Instead, it is more important to compare audience size, image, and response results of other churches that have advertised in various media. Secondly, some churches fail to fully utilize the unique advantages of the medium, especially television. For example, if the church decided on television, then the virtues of the ministry should be demonstrated rather than merely talked through a TV script. Similarly, if billboards are used, avoid copy with a number of words or statements since drivers won't have time to read them.[6]

Finally, another problem that might doom a church's promotional strategies is the church's inability to match its strengths and offerings to the identified needs and preferences of its target market. It is evident that today's churches cannot be everything to everyone. Having identified the needs of the segment of society it hopes to attract, and believing it can provide for those needs, it is imperative that the church successfully match the target market's preferences with the strengths of the church's ministries. Furthermore, it is essential that they can communicate this information to the desired clientele by selecting the right medium.

Promotional Tactics

In their task to successfully communicate the desired information to their target market, church leaders often face serious constraints on their promotional activities, such as limited budgets, resistance internally and externally to the use of certain media, and pressures to avoid controversial messages. In addition, church leaders must deal with the diverse goals of retaining existing members and persuading others to join the church. Thus, it is imperative that church leaders choose the promotional methods that will most effectively accomplish these objectives yet remain within their budget constraints.

To begin with, many churches need to move beyond the established practice of limiting their promotional activities to the placement of ads in the telephone book or putting a sign on the church grounds or possibly placing an ad in the newspaper (again, on the religion page with all the other church ads). While signs, telephone ads, and copycat newspaper ads are informative, they do nothing to persuade a potential attendee. Churches tend to be great imitators when it comes to these forms of promotion. However, since the content of these messages is virtually the same, they would likely have little, if any, impact.

On the other hand, research indicates that the most believable and best-remembered form of recommending a church is the personal recommendation of a trusted friend. Basically, the most effective means of getting people to experience what a church has to offer is having someone they know who belongs to the church simply invite them to try it. This "word-of-mouth" advertising builds upon an established relationship which implies that the invitation springs from a credible source.

George Barna is extremely enthusiastic about the effectiveness of personal invitation. Based on a national survey he conducted among unchurched adults, he found that 25% would attend a church if a friend ever took the time to invite them. Based on approximately 70 million unchurched adults in America, this implies that roughly 18 million adults are "waiting" to go to church. If church leaders can instill in their members the vision of church growth and convince them that they are the actual marketers of the church, this could be a very effective and inexpensive means of attracting new members.[7]

"Word-of-mouth" advertising ties in directly with the P of product in a church's marketing mix. As stated previously, if one of the key aspects of the product of the church is the offering of relationships with others, then it is logical that the best way to promote a church is through the development and growth of meaningful relationships with others. It follows, therefore, that if members of a church perceive the relationship with others in the church as being supportive and meaningful and also believe their personal relationship with God is being strengthened, then one can assure that these individuals would be more likely to invite their friends and neighbors to attend church with them and hopefully enjoy the same benefits they found enjoyable. It is logical that if church members are satisfied with the "product" offered by the church, then they are certainly more apt to consider inviting others, who may only be waiting for an invitation to attend.

Aside from personal invitation, there are often promotional factors that are also feasible for their communication objectives. For example, some churches have found some success in using direct mail. William Novelli suggested that direct mail has some key advantages for nonprofit organizations. First, it can be very focused: it can achieve maximum impact on a specific target market. Assuming a church has identified a specific segment of the community it seeks to pursue in demographic terms, the mailings can be directed to householders that contain such people. Secondly, direct mail can be private and confidential, a major benefit for religious organizations, whose messages are often perceived as very personal matters. Third, costs per contact and costs per response can often be very low, which again is appealing to religious organizations with very low budgets. Finally, results are often quite measurable, and this can help make marketing programs more accountable.[8]

A more nontraditional way of introducing people to a church is sponsoring a community event. Such a practice gives the visitors something of value the very first time they come in contact with the church but in a very nonthreatening setting. Similarly, events geared for children can also be beneficial. If done properly, the kids enjoy the activities, the parents who accompanied their children see the joy and excitement experienced by the kids, and come away with perhaps a positive feeling toward the sponsoring church. However, it is critical for the church to be able to transfer any newly generated interest in the church and goodwill resulting from the event into the next step — a visit to the church.

One church that used the community event process to great advantage is North Coast Presbyterian Church in California. It began an annual series of events called Kidsfest, in which several weekends are devoted to serving the needs of the community. The church has utilized the events as an opportunity to gain community exposure and to position itself as being in touch with the interests of young people and capable of putting together a program of events that will help parents nurture their children.[9]

If a church is sponsoring some community event, it certainly would be advantageous for them to also contact the local media and perhaps invite them to the event — in essence, obtaining needed publicity to generate community awareness. If the media sends a reporter to cover the event, the free exposure could be invaluable. Similarly, by getting news releases published or having feature articles written about the church and its activities, the church can gain enormous benefits because the dissemination of the information by the media appears to have their stamp of approval — lending a degree of credibility. Church leaders need to remember that the media has a profound impact on what people believe and the lifestyles they embrace.

The combination of a church-sponsored event along with coverage and publicity by the local media could be a powerful marketing tool. The news releases regarding the event or even describing the church itself will hopefully attract some reader's *attention*. Secondly, the media exposure could stimulate some reader's *interest* in the event and/or the church, leading ideally to the *desire* to attend. Finally, the desire to attend, again either the event and/or the church, will hopefully lead to the desired *action* — actual attendance. The AIDA theory (attention - interest - desire - action) is an important goal for any promotional strategies and is certainly very applicable to describing what churches are hoping to accomplish (Figure 7.3).

While the previously mentioned tactics — personal invitations, direct mailing, sponsored events, news releases — are effective, yet relatively inexpensive methods, some churches may be fortunate to have a sufficient budget to engage the mass media in an attempt to attract new members. George Barna determined that evaluations of reactions to church advertising clearly indicates that most people believe advertising is an appropriate activity. However, when comparing church advertising, as a whole, to advertising from other industries, church ads were rated lower than all other types. People generally felt that church ads were not interesting, memorable, or persuasive.[10]

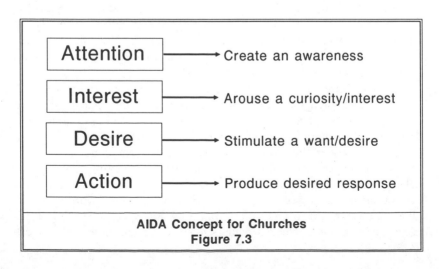

Attention   ⟶ Create an awareness

Interest   ⟶ Arouse a curiosity/interest

Desire   ⟶ Stimulate a want/desire

Action   ⟶ Produce desired response

AIDA Concept for Churches
Figure 7.3

It is estimated the Americans are being bombarded by about 2000 messages per day. Unfortunately, most church ads do not break through the competitive clutter and attract people's attention. Martin Marty points out: "A religious group that offers no presentation of itself in a competitive, complex society will go undiscovered — or if it is already known — it will wane and disappear. The question is not 'will church advertise?' but 'How?'[11]

Again, consider the majority of newspaper ads for churches. Very unimaginative, these ads list the church's name, address and telephone number, pastor's name, times of the service, and perhaps the title of the sermon. These ads are generally placed on the page or two devoted to religion in the Saturday edition of the newspaper. Most likely, these bland, copycat ads are basically only reaching the people who are already religious and have a church home. It is questionable how effective this type of advertising can be.

The problem is that church ads, whether in the newspaper, radio, or television, compete directly with all the other messages urging consumers to react in a prescribed manner. It is essential that all those churches who consider using the mass media understand its complications, costs, and uncertainties. More importantly, church leaders need to determine the expected impact of these media sources.

In his study of successful, growing congregations, Barna discovered that advertising tended to be "informative" rather than "persuasive." Because they were promoting religion upon a different medium (word-of-mouth) to achieve persuasion, they used traditional forms of advertising primarily to build awareness. For example, one church with an $8 million annual budget was spending less than $20,000 on advertising, but still realizing 14% annual growth in attendance.[12] The lesson from these successful, growing congregations is that advertising does have a role in the church's promotion mix and that role is primarily to generate an awareness of the church and perhaps what differentiates it from other local churches. However, what is needed to complement this initial awareness and provide a more persuasive message will be the "promotion" done by its members through word-of-mouth, extending personal invitations to friends and neighbors, inviting them to share the spiritual, emotional, and social relationships they have developed at the church.

The communication goals of a church should be twofold. First, it needs to develop effective retention communication capabilities to keep its current members abreast of the church's vision, opportunities, expectations, and mission. Like any for-profit organization, a church needs to keep its current customers satisfied and keep them informed as to what the church is up to. Second, a church needs also to focus on acquisition communication strategies in order to attract newcomers and eventually persuade them to become active members of the congregation.

As mentioned previously, there are estimated to be over 70 million "unchurched" Americans. This represents a huge potential market for any marketing-oriented church that desires to be sensitive and responsive to the needs of this untapped segment. If such a church can effectively reach these people and inform them of the church's offerings, opportunities, and progress, and be able to demonstrate how these features can match their spiritual and/or emotional needs, then this type of church may enjoy unprecedented growth in the 90s.

Implications

Certainly, mass media ads conveying something interesting, or informing about a special event, or even indicating how the church is unique and different, and which are believable can be somewhat effective. However, I believe that since most churches operate on severely constrained budgets, they should consider the previously mentioned tactics which have been highly effective for some churches and are relatively inexpensive. Most importantly, a church should not overlook its most important means of communication — its own members. By considering every member a potential "marketer" of the church, church leaders need to successfully communicate to its members the vision of the church, its goals and objectives, and ideally energize them to willingly participate and become actively involved in the successful accomplishment of the church's mission. Certainly, a member's sincere invitation to others to come visit will be a much more powerful promotional tool than a small ad in the newspaper or a 30 second spot on local television.

Endnotes

1. Christian H. Lovelock and Charles B. Weinberg, *Public and Nonprofit Marketing,* Redwood City, CA, The Scientific Press, 1989, p. 297.

2. George Barna, *Church Marketing,* Ventura, CA, Regal Books, 1992, p. 185.

3. *Ibid.*

4. George Barna, *Marketing the Church,* Colorado Springs, CO, Navpress, 1988, p. 139.

5. Barna, *Marketing the Church,* p. 141.

6. Shawchuck, et al., *Marketing for Congregations,* p. 309.

7. Barna, *Marketing the Church,* p. 111.

8. William D. Novelli, "Social Issues and Direct Marketing: What's the Connection?" Presentation to the Annual Conference of the Direct Mail/Marketing Association, Los Angeles, CA, March 12, 1981.

9. Barna, *Marketing the Church,* p. 116.

10. Barna, *Church Marketing,* p. 195.

11. Martin E. Marty, "Sunday Mass and the Media," *Across the Board,* May 1987, p. 56.

12. Barna, *User Friendly Churches,* pp. 101-102.

8

Direct Mail:
An Appropriate Strategy for Churches

Introduction

One of the fastest growing aspects of communication employed by both profit and nonprofit organizations to reach their target markets is direct marketing. Direct marketing has many definitions, and in the past has gone by other names: direct mail, mail order, and direct response. "Direct Mail" is, in fact, a promotional medium in which the mails are used to disseminate messages. These communications can come in various forms and sizes: letters, postcards, leaflets, catalogs, and coupons. "Mail order" does its promotion through any medium, such as television, magazines, and newspapers. The mail order technique is basically a method of product distribution. Finally, "direct response" is a name given to an advertising technique that elicits an immediate response, such as an order or inquiry, or a visit to a store or showroom.

Direct mailing incorporates all three of these concepts. The most widely accepted definition was drawn up by a committee of the Direct Marketing Association (DMA). They defined direct marketing as "an interacting system of marketing which uses one or more advertising media to effect a measurable response and/or transaction at any location." The DMA definition can be simplified by employing the concepts of media usage and direct response. In essence, direct marketing is simply impersonal promotion, in the sense of not being face-to-face, which seeks to evoke direct action.[1]

While some profit and nonprofit organizations may easily utilize all of the three main concepts of direct marketing, direct mail appears to be a feasible tool for churches to utilize in order to more effectively communicate with its desired target market. Unfortunately, most religious organizations have not considered using direct mail as a means to contact their constituencies in spite of the successful uses of other organizations. Direct mail is the "heart" of the direct marketing industry. It is the third largest advertising medium, next to newspapers and television.

The purpose of this chapter is to offer logical support for the use of direct mail by churches in an attempt to more effectively reach their desired publics and also to more effectively communicate their message to these segments. In the past decade, the nature of communication has changed radically. Although television, radio, newspapers, and magazine advertising formerly represented the dominant means of reaching an audience, more and more advertisers are moving away from reliance on these mass media. Instead, they are turning to "targeted media": communication vehicles that enable them to reach a more narrowly defined, concentrated audience.[2] As other organizations achieve success with direct mail, it is certainly appropriate for churches to examine this tool, understand not only the benefits, but also the limitations of direct mail, and consider developing strategies for a direct mail campaign.

Benefits of Direct Mail

As mentioned previously, a marketing-oriented church should be responsive to the needs of the segment of society it hopes to attract. As a result, church leaders must strive to determine effective ways to communicate their offerings to their target market. Again, many church leaders have been reluctant to consider using direct mail as a means to communicate information. Part of the hesitation towards direct mail stems from church leaders' belief that direct mail won't work and/or it will cost too much. Similarly, some church leaders may simply be unaware as to what direct mail is, how it can be utilized, and what benefits can be expected.

To influence church leaders to become more receptive towards the use of direct mail, it is essential that they first become aware of the actual performance of other direct mail studies. To begin with, Walter Mueller claims that based on solid statistical studies, direct mail gives the "most" results for the "least" time, effort, and money. He offers an article by Robert Enstad, which was syndicated by the Chicago Tribute Service, that supported his argument. Enstad indicated that while sales from direct mail marketing are growing at an estimated 15% each year, over-the-counter sales are increasing at a rate of only about 6% each year.[3]

Another objection one may have regarding direct mail is that our mailboxes are filled with "junk" mail every day so no one would read direct mail correspondence. Ensted provided another interesting fact that would counter such an argument. He indicates the Direct Mail Marketing Association (DMMA) has instituted several services for those who receive so-called junk mail. Since some people don't appreciate receiving all this unsolicited mail, the DMMA has provided a way for names to be deleted from mailing lists. They have also provided an appropriate service for those who would like to have their names placed on more lists.

Enstad, quoting a representative of DMMA, wrote: "We had about 80,000 requests from persons wanting to get on or off mailing lists. About 20,000 persons wanted less mail. 60,000 asked to receive more mail. Such findings will hopefully expose the fallacy that direct mail won't wash."[4]

In addition to overcoming some of the common misconceptions of direct mail, it is equally important that religious leaders be informed of the definite benefits that a direct mail strategic campaign can provide. For example, direct mail provides several important advantages for nonprofit organizations:[5]

(1) Direct mail tends to be very focused: it can achieve maximum impact on a specific target market.

If a church has segmented the market and chosen an appropriate segment(s) to pursue, then direct mail would be an ideal way to focus a church's communication efforts on its intended target.

(2) Direct mail can be private and confidential.

This feature would be extremely advantageous for churches since most people perceive religious matters as very personal. Direct mail would not be as threatening as a telemarketing approach or home visitation. It obviously would be less intrusive, allowing the recipient to read the message at his/her own convenience and privately decide whether or not to pursue the church's invitation.

(3) The cost per contact and cost per response can often be very low.

This would be a key advantage to churches with limited budgets, still allowing them to reach their intended target market in a cost effective manner.

(4) Direct mail results are often clearly measurable, and this can help make marketing programs more accountable.

Unlike other forms of advertising where the results are often difficult to truly measure and the desired responses often quite delayed, direct mail provides a quantifiable response so church members can easily measure the impact of their efforts. A successful direct mail venture can also be used in the future to justify additional campaigns, since the success can be objectively described.

(5) Small-scale tests of proposed strategies are very feasible with direct mail.

In fact, direct mail is an ideal field test vehicle. A number of marketing factors can be varied over several mailings and the results compared to baseline measures.

Direct mail offers churches great flexibility in the design of their desired messages, allowing them the ability to determine "what works the best." Similarly, the scope of the campaign can be easily adjusted to remain within the budgeting constraints of the church. The possibilities are quite extensive in that churches could try to determine the impact of a variety of different messages or themes and determine what type of approach has the greatest impact.

(6) The effectiveness of direct mail can be assessed directly in terms of behavior (for example, requests and inquiries), whereas other media assessments usually require attitude and awareness indicators, which are generally faced with measurement problems.

The advantages of direct mail identified by Novelli provide a solid rationale for their usage by churches. However, it would be imperative that the church has a clear focus on exactly who it hopes to attract. A mass mailing to everyone in the immediate community would not only be extremely expensive, but most certainly a waste of a church's resources. The use of direct mail clearly implies market segmentation by the church. Having identified the specific segment of the church it hopes to pursue, a direct mail campaign can be directed only to those householders that contain such people. Although the cost of using a focused, targeted mail campaign usually winds up being higher per household than is true for a mass mail campaign (i.e., mailing to every household in the targeted geographic area), the budget can be stretched further and generally reaps greater dividends.

Barna offers the following chart to demonstrate a comparison of how a mailing to all 50,000 households in one community would have cost a church $17,800; a mailing sent to the 10,000 householders most likely to have an interest in the church's message was $4,310.

Cost Component	Cost per Thousand	Community-wide Mailing (50K-HH)	Targeted-household Mailing (10K-HH)
Brochure	$200 at 50k $250 at 10k	$10,000	$2,500
Mailing List	$40 for all $65 for segments	$2,000	$650
Handling	$5	$250	$50
Postage	$111	$5,550	$1,100
Total Cost		**$17,000**	**$4,310**
Cost per household		**$0.356**	**$0.431**

**A Comparison of the Cost of a Mass Mailing and a Targeted Mailing
Figure 8.1**

Barna points out that for the targeted approach, the cost per household was higher. This was a result of the cost of printing the brochures, which was higher due to the smaller print run, and the more expensive mailing list because it was more selective. The choices facing the church are as follows: It could spend $17,800 to send a brochure to each household one time. It could spend $4,310 for a single exposure to the households most likely to be interested in the message being communicated. Or, it could spend $17,210 (still less than the cost of a single community-wide mailing) to reach the target audience four times, either with the same message or different brochures, knowing that multiple exposure to a message increases the likelihood of impact.[6]

A well-designed message addressing the felt needs of the intended target market can be effective and could be influential in encouraging these individuals to visit the church. In addition, the church that implements direct mail as part of its communication strategy may also enjoy other, intangible benefits. Walter Mueller believes that a consistent direct mail program will give both the pastor and the church a reputation for being progressive. It will also promote an image of an active church. Similarly, it will communicate a sense of strength and unity with the church. It can also be used to call attention to and promote interest in the programs of the church. Finally, Mueller claims that a direct mail program will clearly communicate to everyone on the mailing list that this is a church that is serious about its God-given responsibility to reach people for Christ.

While this section has discussed the main direct and indirect benefits that direct marketing can provide a church, it is important to realize that since the typical household now receives in excess of 1,500 unsolicited pieces of mail each year, it will take a polished, professional piece to cut through the clutter and make such a significant impression that it will alter an established behavior pattern. Similarly, the return rate — i.e., the percentage of householders who respond to the mailing — does not exceed 1%.[7] Thus, direct mail is certainly no panacea. If done poorly or amateurishly, the results could be disastrous and a waste of a church's precious resources. The next section will discuss some of the cautions and limitations that church leaders should also be aware of.

Limitations of Direct Mail

As mentioned previously, the typical household is bombarded with more and more unsolicited pieces of mail each year. Unless careful attention is given to a church's direct mail program, its mailings may easily be lost among all the other pieces of mail reaching the targeted household.

A fundamental concern for church leaders considering a direct mail campaign has to be a segmentation of the population. It is critical that churches clearly identify the specific target market(s) to whom they believe their church can most effectively address these individuals' needs.

The problem is that many churches have basically utilized a "mass marketing" approach when a single appeal was made to an undifferentiated mass market. Such an approach pays no attention to differences in people's needs, preferences, or behavior, and is primarily concerned with meeting the organization's own needs. The bottom line is that a church cannot be all things to all people. It is not feasible for a church to try to satisfy each need of each individual who comes into contact with that church.

Similarly, a church should not expect every household in a specified geographic area to have an interest in the church and its activities. In essence, rather than trying to reach every household, a church needs to target its limited resources to reach a specific segment of the population. Church leaders need to understand that different segments of the population respond to different ministry opportunities, and focusing one's communication efforts on a specific target group allows for a more efficient attraction of that market.

Having identified the specific market segment it hopes to attract, another critical concern of a direct marketing program is that the message conveyed in the literature is appropriate and well-received by the intended group. If the message conveyed turns people off, is misunderstood, or has absolutely no effect on the recipient, then the entire campaign could be a huge waste of time and money.

For example, one church put out a mailing just before Easter. The timing seemed appropriate — a good time to search for church visitors, since many people wander into churches during the traditional holy days of Christmas and Easter. Amazingly, not a single person from the 40,000 households reached by the mailing came to visit that church. On examining the materials, it became apparent why nobody showed up. Who wants to be told that they are sinners and will go to hell if they don't change their lifestyle? That was essentially what the brochure told people. The colors were dark, the message was one of fear and guilt, and the church was in a really unaccessible location. In this situation, Barna concluded the problem was not the medium, but instead the message.[8]

Direct Mail Tactics

If a church's direct mail campaign is to be effective, a great deal of thought and planning will be required in terms of the message to be sent. Church leaders considering a direct mail program as part of their overall marketing strategy will need to be able to answer the following questions regarding the use of direct mail: What, To Whom, How, When, and How Many.

What

Since direct mail is a form of marketing communication, church leaders need to establish some clear-cut objectives as to what they want to accomplish through the use of a direct mail company. Are they intending to use direct mail to simply make members in the community aware of the church, as might be the case if the church is new or has moved location? Or are they trying to convey such a message that will hopefully stimulate the recipient's interest leading to a change in attitude and/or behavior? A direct mail program geared to creating awareness would convey a very different message than one desiring to change one's behavior. Thus, it is first critical that church leaders clearly identify the key objective of the direct mail campaign. Poorly clarified objectives will likely lead to ineffective messages, thus resulting in minimal impact.

To Whom

Just as the church leaders must be clear as to the desired objective to be accomplished, so must they be focused on the intended target audience. As mentioned previously, a "mass marketing" approach is no longer feasible for today's churches. They must have a clear vision as to the type(s) of people they are trying to attract. Is it people in certain age groups (baby boomers, baby busters), lifestyles, those possessing certain needs, couples, singles, or newcomers? Certain groups will be more responsive to direct mail than others. By not having a clear identity of their target market, a church is wasting its precious resources and will result in an ineffective and inefficient use of direct mail.

Having selected its desired target market, it is then necessary for the church to develop an appropriate mailing list. Several outside services can be the source of highly tailored prospect lists defined by schools, occupation area, socioeconomic status of the neighborhood, patronage of a particular product, service or outlets, and so on. Whenever time permits, new rented lists should be tested with small mailings to see if they are productive before the campaign continues with the unknown target list. However, the best lists would most likely be those containing the addresses of people with whom the organization already has some form of contact.[9] This infers that it is critical for churches to maintain good internal records — keeping track of those who perhaps responded to past mailing, who made inquiries in the past, or who have actually visited the church on some occasion. Members of the congregation could also be asked who they might know — friends, relatives co-workers — who might be interested in the church and its activities. These names could also be included in the mailing.

How

Having defined the objective of the direct mail campaign and selected the specific target market they are trying to reach, church leaders must now decide on how to most effectively convey their intended message. Obviously, they must try to develop the most compelling and intriguing message possible to attract such individuals since the church's direct mail piece will be competing with all the other unsolicited mail for the individual's attention. While different messages will require different approaches, listed below are some factors to consider in developing the direct mail piece.

Style — Many church letters are quite dry and boring. They provide the basic information, but do little to motivate the recipient. Jerry Huntsinger, who wrote the letters that raised the millions of dollars necessary to build Robert Schuller's Crystal Cathedral, suggests that to get results by direct mail, one's style must be simple and homey. Use stories, short words (60% or more should be five letters or less).[10]

Color — The use of color can add both to the attractiveness and effectiveness of direct mail pieces. Color can be used to add life to the copy and may help convey certain ideas that may be used to advantage. According to tests performed by the Direct Mail Advertising Associates, the most legible copy is produced by means of black ink on yellow paper. It is recommended to use nothing but black ink for lengthy paragraphs, since other colors create eyestrain, which causes the reader to be psychologically "turned off" to the message you are trying to communicate.

Content — Church leaders need to ensure that the mailing contains all the necessary information. Has anything been left out: who, what when, where, and why? Similarly, the direct mail piece needs to be edited for accuracy. Are there any grammatical, punctuation, or spelling errors? Also, is the information provided accurate? The dates and locations need to be given accurately.

Clarity — Since the direct mail piece will be competing with all the other unsolicited mail received by the recipient, it is critical to avoid being too wordy. It will probably be necessary to edit and re-edit the message, striving to be as concise as possible. Similarly, it is essential that the message is written as clearly as possible. It shouldn't breed confusion or misunderstanding among the recipients. Without being patronizing, the message should be written in such a way that it will be understandable to all who read it.

Uniqueness — This factor is somewhat of an intangible. Again, the church's direct mail piece is merely one of many the recipient must wade through. Thought should be given as to how to make the church's piece stand out and catch the attention of the individual. Some suggestions might include the use of illustrations or drawings to enhance the appearance of the copy. Another possibility might be the use of humor to try to put the recipient at ease and not feel threatened by a religious message. A catchy phrase, a small limerick, or some subtle attempts at humor may add spice to the message. By catching the reader's attention early on, this may ensure that the full message is actually read.

Finally, to help pinpoint potential problems or areas of miscommunication, it is recommended that each direct mail piece be pretested. Obviously, once the piece is sent out, the church can do very little to clarify any issues, change the copy, or reinforce the intended message. It would be feasible to try utilizing sample target audience members that are representative of the constituency the church is trying to reach. Pretesting can be helpful to examine whether the intended message is being understood by the recipients, whether there are any areas of confusion, whether any pertinent information is lacking, and whether the message is persuading or threatening. Pretesting is relatively inexpensive, does not take up too much time, and can be extremely helpful in fine-tuning the direct mail offering so that it can accomplish the intended objectives.

When

Once the direct mail piece has been pretested and any necessary modifications made, church leaders need to then determine the timing of the mailings. Walter Mueller believes that since many people are likely to attend church on Easter or Christmas, a mailing should be done prior to either of these seasons. An unchurched family, thinking of attending a church on one of these two holy days, is quite likely to choose to attend a church because of the mail they have received. If they plan to attend a church, it will likely be one they are aware of.[11]

The timing of the mailing is critical. If one receives notice of a special service or church activity many weeks prior to the event, the person is likely to put it aside and most likely disregard it or forget about it. Similarly, if the message is received a day or two before the event, this may be too sudden, and the individual feels pressured or threatened due to closeness of the activity and ultimately disregards it. Ideally, the direct mail piece should arrive 4-6 days before the date of the event. This timing is a "happy medium" between the two extremes and allows the individual time to process the information, evaluate the message, and ample time to make plans to attend if so inclined.

How Many

Another issue is whether to rely on only one piece of mail to accomplish the church's objectives. It is obvious that multiple exposure to a message will increase the likelihood of impact. However, much will depend on the availability of funding for such a multiple-mailing strategy. Walter Mueller firmly believes that one piece is not enough. His church has used a series of four mailings prior to Easter quite successfully. The first three mailings consisted of what could be called flyers, while the fourth was an eight-page tabloid or newspaper. They were mailed at two-week intervals, with the first to reach the recipients prior to the beginning of Lent, and the last to be received just before the beginning of Holy Week.[12]

Finally, like any other means of communication, it is essential that some type of feedback exist to inform the church what works or doesn't work. In using a direct mail program, a church leader should learn from each mailing what works or doesn't work in the mailing design itself. As mentioned previously, one of the main benefits of direct mail is the ability to clearly measure the results and objectively assess the impact of the mailing. Similarly, direct mail's flexibility allows for experimentation with different messages, use of colors, unique approaches, etc., to determine which approach is most effective.

Feedback from a direct mail program can also tell something about the respondent. Tom McCabe of International Marketing Group notes: "You know exactly who responds and why. . . . Every time someone responds to a mailing, you learn something about that person. Direct marketing is very efficient because eventually you will be able to know what kind of return to expect on every marketing dollar you spend."[13]

Implications

Direct mail is one of the fastest growing areas of marketing. Its effectiveness has been demonstrated in many profit and nonprofit firms. It is, therefore, logical that churches should also consider direct mail as one way to reach out to their desired constituents and effectively communicate their message.

In spite of the limitations and cautions of direct mail, I firmly believe that direct mail can be an effective tool as part of a church's communication strategies. However, the effective use of direct mail demands that the church is marketing-centered, has carefully identified the segment of the population it believes it can most effectively serve, and is aware of the needs of this targeted group it hopes to attract.

Endnotes

1. Herbert Katzenstein and William S. Sacks, *Direct Marketing*. Columbus, OH: Charles E. Merrill Publishing Company, 1986.

2. George Barna, *Church Marketing*. Ventura, CA: Regal Books, 1992, p. 195.

3. Walter Mueller, *Direct Marketing Ministry*. Nashville, TN: Abingdon Press, 1989, p. 18.

4. *Ibid.*, p. 19.

5. William D. Novelli, "Social Issues and Direct Marketing: What's the Connection?", Annual Conference of the Direct Mail Marketing Association, Los Angeles, California, March 23, 1991.

6. George Barna, *Church Marketing,* p. 196.

7. George Barna, *Marketing the Church.* Colorado Springs, CO: Navpress, 1988, p. 115.

8. *Ibid.*

9. Norman Shawchuck, Philip Kotler, Bruce Wren, Gustave Rath, *Marketing for Congregations,* Nashville, TN: Abingdon Press, 1992, p. 295.

10. Walter Mueller, *Direct Mail Ministry,* pp. 45-46.

11. *Ibid.,* p. 67.

12. *Ibid.,* p. 67.

13. Norman Shawchuck, et al., *Marketing for Congregations,* 1992, p. 296.

9

Attracting Baby Boomers Back to the Church

Introduction

Without doubt, the most closely watched segment of the American population is the baby boomer generation — those individuals born between 1946 and 1964 who number over 75 million. This segment has been under the watchful eye of marketers for years since the sheer size of the group and their increased spending power has certainly made them a very appropriate target market.

While so many organizations have strived to provide the types of products and services that hopefully meet the needs and wants of baby boomers, churches have been very slow in recognizing the somewhat unique spiritual needs of this large segment, and secondly, have done very little in providing the types of worship and programs that would best appeal to baby boomers.

To a marketing-oriented church, this generation represents a huge, virtually untapped potential target market. Those churches desiring to grow and attract more people into a relationship with God need to consider strategies and tactics that will identify the spiritual and emotional needs of baby boomers and then design the types of worship, services, programs, and offerings that most effectively address these needs.

The baby boomer will likely be the most important source of church growth in the coming decade. First, this segment of the population will reach the age cohort at which life begins to stabilize (job, hours, family, finances) and attachment to traditional values and institutions become more likely. To many people in the 30-50 age bracket, church membership is a symbol of belonging, a way of becoming an accepted and ingrained part of the community.

Second, many adults in the baby-boom cohort have apparently "burned out" on popular culture to the extent that religion is now assuming a more important place in their lives. Since 1982, the proportion of adults who claim that religion is "very important" and returned to church has jumped nearly 20% — with much of that increase a result of the renewed interest among baby boomers.[1]

As an indication of the importance and potential of the generation for churches, *Time* featured a cover article entitled "The Generation That Forgot God." Ironically, the article states that of the generation born after World War II, 95% received a religious upbringing, and had they been awed like their parents before them, the churches and synagogues of their childhood would be thriving. However, what has happened is that a large percentage of baby boomers have left the church in record numbers.

According to Wade Clark Roof, who has studied boomers' attitudes toward God, about a third have never strayed from the church. Another one-fourth of boomers are defectors who have returned to religious practice — at least for now. The returnees are usually less tied to tradition and less dependable as church members than loyalists.

The returnees are still vastly outnumbered by the 42% of baby boomers who remain dropouts from formal religion. Roof's study, however, found that most said they felt their children should receive religious training — creating an opportunity that some churches are rushing to meet. Two potent events that might draw dropouts back to the fold are having children and facing at mid-life a personal or a career crisis that reminds boomers of the need for moorings.[2]

The fact that such a large percentage of this segment of the population remains "unchurched" is a severe threat to many churches' survival. As mentioned previously, mainline Protestants — the traditional denominations such as Methodist, Presbyterian, Episcopalian, and the United Church of Christ — have lost more than a quarter of their members in the last two decades. Growth has even slowed for Southern Baptists, probably the chief beneficiaries of America's move to the Sunbelt and fundamentalism.

Meanwhile, the existing mainline members are graying. Fast. The average age of members of American Baptist Churches was 61 in 1991; 38% of United Methodists in 1990 were over 50, compared with 26% of the U.S. population at large; and a 1988 study of Presbyterians showed that because nearly half the active lay members were headed for retirement, money problems will be "almost beyond belief." Other mainline agencies face a similar pocketbook crunch.[3]

It is encouraging that some of the previously "unchurched" baby boomers are finding spiritual homes again and some churches are growing at phenomenal rates. Dramatic gains elsewhere in Protestantism — mostly in free-standing, interdenominational churches — have equalled mainstream losses. It appears that while the market for religion hasn't necessarily shrunk, market-share has changed dramatically.

Why does one church thrive while another struggles? Why does one type of church appeal to baby boomers searching for a spiritual home while others are apparently unsuccessful in attracting those from this generation? As the baby boomer generation represents such a huge potential and challenge to a marketing-oriented church, the purpose of this chapter is threefold. First, the attitudinal and behavioral characteristics of baby boomers will be explored those attributes which differentiate them from their parents' generation. Second, the variety of reasons and explanations why so many baby boomers left the church will be addressed, as well as the various activities and interests they have turned to instead of church. Finally, several practical strategies designed to help a marketing-oriented church attract baby boomers and most effectively satisfy their specific spiritual needs and wants will be discussed.

Characteristics of Baby Boomers

While it is illogical to imply that this huge segment of the population all share the same attributes, there do appear to be certain attitudinal and behavioral characteristics that many baby boomers seem to possess, and these characteristics most definitely differentiate this generation from other segments of the population. Furthermore, these unique characteristics also help explain why today's churches are having difficulty attracting and/or retaining baby boomers.

To begin with, baby boomers are the first Americans who have little or no loyalty to a church or denomination. Similarly, they are the first Americans who feel little or no loyalty to the religion of their parents. When baby boomers turn to the church, they shop for the services they want, much like they shop for items at the supermarket. It's not unusual today to find a baby boomer family attending Sunday School at one church, because it has excellent classes for children, and then going down the street to attend worship services at another church, because it has an outstanding music program and/or preacher.[4]

Ironically, one very striking characteristic of this generation is that the majority began life in religious households. Based on his extensive research on baby boomers, Roof found that virtually all (96%) of those surveyed said they were raised in a religious tradition. As children during the 1950s and 1960s, they were reared within Protestant, Catholic, or Jewish faiths so they would fit into a conformist, pro-religious culture. They attended Sunday School and religion classes in record numbers, and they often were the reason their parents returned to the church. The "religious renewal" of the 1950s was due in part to parents' concerns about the religious education of their children.

In spite of their religious upbringing, most baby boomers usually dropped out of church as soon as they could. Roof found that most (58%) of those with a religious background dropped out for at least two years during their adolescence or young adulthood. Eighty-four percent of Jews dropped out, as did 60% of mainline Protestants, 57% of Catholics, and 54% of conservative Protestants.[5]

Likewise, many baby boomers are anti-organization and anti-institution. Boomers are great participants, but not very good belongers. Church membership will need to be downplayed and replaced with terms and expressions that emphasize participation. As mentioned previously, boomers are very low on denominational loyalty. Due to the busy demands on their time, boomers will more likely connect with a local nondenominational church rather than drive a longer distance to a church of their own denomination.[6]

Another unifying theme which differentiates baby boomers from other age groups is their unique cultural experiences and preferences. This generation is much more than just an actual age span. Baby boomers embody a cultural phenomenon, or set of attitudes and assumptions distinctive to this generation. They are the generation of the Viet Nam War, of the Kent State University tragedy, of the flower people and drugs, of the assassination of President John F. Kennedy, Senator Robert F. Kennedy, and Reverend Martin Luther King, Jr., and of the Watergate Scandal that forced President Richard Nixon to resign in shame.[7]

Roof believes that the tumult of the 1960s and 1970s, the rise of a distinct counterculture, and the massive size of the baby boom generation all combined to create a social atmosphere that questioned the authority of established institutions. He believes this generation gap among believers is still evident in many congregations and especially among the declining Protestant mainline churches.[8]

During this decade, the culture of the baby boomer generation will not only be legitimized, it will also be empowered and unleashed. Baby boomers are just now beginning to flex their muscles and test their strength. That is why most demographers agree that the culture of the boomer generation is just now beginning to dominate U.S. culture and will continue to do so into the next century.

Churches that don't take this baby boom phenomenon into account will look even more antiquated in the years to come.[9] While this generation left the church in record numbers, it is hopeful that they will also return in surprising number. However, before a marketing-oriented church can begin to reach out and minister successfully to the baby boom generation, it must comprehend why so many of this generation willingly left the church, and what activities, interests, or other beliefs they turned to instead. The next section examines some of the apparent reasons.

Abandoning the Church

As stated previously, the overwhelming majority of baby boomers grew up in religious households. Throughout their early years, they were exposed to Sunday Schools, religious classes, and were raised in a religious tradition. While young people have abandoned their churches in the past, it has rarely been in such large numbers. Such a dramatic dropout demands some explanation as to what went wrong. Why did so many of this generation leave the church in spite of their religious upbringing? What did churches do, or perhaps not do, which resulted in this large exodus?

Some believe that one main reason baby boomers have left the church is that they feel the message being delivered from the pulpit is not relevant to them. Some analyses state that many mainline churches are suffering because they have failed to transmit a compelling Christian message to their own children or anybody else. "One thing about Episcopalians, Methodists, and Catholics," says

Margaret Polona, a professor of sociology, "is that people in leadership positions are out of touch with the people in the pews."[10]

Pastors seeking to attract baby boomers must realize that baby boomers are extremely pragmatic about their sermon tastes. William Easum believes that effective pastors replace "ought to" sermons with "how to" sermons. They show how to take what is said on Sunday and use it in hands-on ways Monday through Friday. In order to do this, pastors need a working knowledge of the business world and constant contact with what is going on in the lives of both the members and the unchurched.[11]

Similarly, based on his studies of successful, growing churches, George Barna believes a main reason for the success of the churches he studied was their determination to remain sensitive to the people they were seeking to reach and serve. This meant understanding how people in their community live, and what needs they have which a church might address. It also meant staying informed about how people respond to the church itself, the level of quality with which the church's people, program, director, benefits, opportunities for service and facilities, are impacting the community.[12]

The disillusionment of many baby boomers towards the churches they left points out the difference between a product-driven church and a marketing-oriented church. In a product-driven church, church leaders have a fixed model or vision of what the church should be like, and vigorously implement that vision, regardless of whether or not it addresses the specific spiritual needs of its members. As many baby boomers have rejected the rigid model maintained by the church, church leaders may easily place the blame on the defectors, labeling them as unspiritual, materialistic, uncaring, etc. It is apparent that many baby boomers who have left the church feel that the church's message, structure, environment, or policies do not coincide with their spiritual, emotional, and/or relationship needs.

On one hand, it is encouraging that many baby boomers have a desire to return to a real spiritual home. However, in their spiritual quest, many of this generation are unable to relate to a church culture dominated by their parents. Ironically, though only one generation apart chronologically, these generations may be light years apart culturally.

Part of the problem confronting baby boomers searching for a church is that the predominant cultural vitality of the church rests with the parents of baby boomers. Members from this generation are generally the designated leaders of their church, and they have very different value systems and are not motivated in the same way.

Seldom are baby boomers welcomed into the power structure of the church. They are allowed to teach Sunday School and work in the various programs of the church, but are seldom found on power committees.

It is imperative that today's churches realize that times have changed. There are now more persons in America who are either not associated with any religion whatsoever, or who are connected to a religious tradition other than the traditional Catholic, Orthodox, Protestant, and Jewish faiths. The problem is compounded by the fact that the baby boom generation is the first generation of Americans who have not simply "bought" the faith and ecclesiastical traditions of their parents.

It is also unfortunate for churches that many of the baby boomers who dropped out of religion have not returned to church. These religious dropouts claim over one-third of boomers. Religious dropouts have made a permanent change in America's social landscape.[13]

However, the good news is that a quiet revolution is taking place that is changing not only the religious habits of millions of Americans but the way churches go about recruiting to keep their doors open. Increasing numbers of baby boomers who left the fold years ago are turning religious again, but many are traveling from church to church or faith to faith, in essence sampling the various religious offerings.[14]

In light of this renewed interest in religion exhibited by baby boomers, some churches have enjoyed dramatic growth in membership. Why does one church thrive while another struggles? What should a marketing-oriented church do to try to most effectively satisfy the specific needs of this elusive and complex generation? The next section discusses certain strategies that may help attract those baby boomers searching for a religious home.

Strategies to Attract Baby Boomers

By ancient tradition, a church is designed to celebrate the glory of God. Now, however, it must do many other things as well. Many church leaders have realized that the best way to lure baby boomers back to the church is to first understand the unique characteristics, values, needs and wants of this generation and then try to make certain changes in their vision, ministry, offerings, preaching, and worship that cater to their diverse lifestyles. While change may be threatening to some church leaders, the suggested changes should not dilute the basic substance of Christianity, and these changes can be accomplished without abandoning any of the basic tenets of Christianity as defined by the various denominations. The following topics are possible areas where churches can make changes in order to appeal, attract, and retain baby boomers. This list is by no means all inclusive, but does include some key areas where churches can make an impact.

Informality

For example, to many baby boomers, "formality is phony" and these boomers searching for a church aren't looking for formalized institutions, but informality with meaning. Likewise, many baby boomers remain jeans-wearing people, partly because they are comfortable and partly because they are commenting on casualness. Baby boomers attending a church don't want to be judged for what they are wearing, but appreciated for what they are.

Even though baby boomers are coming back to church, they aren't willing to attend formalized institutions. "Traditional" is a bad word to boomers. But "stable" is not. Stable congregations who build on a caring environment that is heavy on the personal touch and participation will have ample opportunity to see people who are 30-something join their order.[15]

Stressing Relationships

One of the main aspects of the "product" of a marketing-oriented church is the offering of relationships. Firstly, the church encourages its members to develop a lifelong relationship with Jesus Christ. Secondly, the church also offers a relationship with others in the church. The interpersonal relationship with a church can provide support, encouragement, friendship, and a sharing of thoughts and ideas that may be so important to many baby boomers.

Sociologists indicate that one of the consequences of the rushed, hectic lifestyles of many boomers is a sense of loneliness. The church can offer a solution to the aloneness so many are seeking to escape. Based on his research of successful, growing churches, George Barna discussed that many people were attracted to a church because of the possibility of meeting new people and becoming part of a group with similar interests, concerns, and background. In addition, he found that most new church members first attended a specific church because they were invited by someone they knew and trusted. Similarly, one of the most compelling reasons people identified for sticking with their current church was that their friends — many of whom they met only after becoming active at the church — were also members of that church. To these people, the church had become a part of the extended family.[16]

Since so many boomers are single and many mid-life couples may have been relocated several times, they are likely looking to connect with others, and a church providing an opportunity to develop relationships with others may represent a means of being with other people who share common interests and needs.

Families

One of the major events that appears to bring dropouts back to the church is having children. Since baby boomers are having children of their own in growing numbers, they're beginning to look for help to establish values that they wish to communicate to their child. Many boomers are uncomfortable with the gap that exists between their values and their lifestyle. Churches can help narrow this gap by (1) providing values clarification courses that help boomer parents read a precise understanding of their values and how those values affect their families; (2) providing resources and opportunities that help families reclaim their role as the primary source for transmitting values from one generation to another; and (3) publicizing that the church cares about families.[17]

Another big concern for boomer parents searching for a church is the availability of quality child care. Smaller congregations have found that a simple way of encouraging baby boomers to attend services is to provide daycare for infants and toddlers. Easum believes that babies boomers are absent in many mainstream churches because of the deplorable conditions of most nurseries. He advises churches to fix up the nursery before baby boomers arrive, not after. Otherwise, they visit and never return.[18] Baby boomer parents have fewer children today and value quality child care. They are particular where they leave their children. Church leaders need to understand the need for a clean, inviting nursery, staffed by paid people, and open every time the church has a function.

Singles

In contrast, another demographic trend that churches really need to become aware of is the rapidly growing singles' population. Married couples with children, in 1976, were 40% of all American householders, but now they are only 28%. Today, the single population, with or without children, is in excess of 50% of all adults above the age of 18. This phenomena is a new reality for the 1990s. Couples with children will no longer dominate the pews. Church leaders must also realize that singleness is a very complex and difficult issue because it represents numerous age categories and life situations.

Unfortunately, many churches aren't prepared for this aspect of the baby boomer world because of certain biases against singles. These biases within the Christian community have prevented churches from integrating and involving single people in the life and ministry of the congregation.

In order to attract singles, a church must first present singles in a positive light. It is essential to dispel any stereotypical myths of singles and make sure those biases disappear.[19] More importantly, church leaders must address the felt needs of singles in the congregation and provide them with opportunities for worship and fellowship. Churches should also be extremely sensitive to the needs of single-parent families. Finally, involving singles in leadership is another important step for every congregation that desires to reach out to baby boomers.

Role of Women

Similarly, another segment of the population that has been limited in their role in churches has been women. The typical unchurched baby boomer assumes that the formal church is so male-oriented that it is closed to women functioning in any capacity equal with men. This contrasts with the assumption that boomers believe women need to be represented in leadership. This generation will judge the church's morality by the participation of women. Where women are not recognized in leadership positions, those congregations will be judged to be morally invalid in the hearts of some, and at least a little out-of-touch in the hearts of others.[20] For example, baby boomers visiting a church and noting that no women are leaders or involved in any way will evaluate church leadership accordingly, and perhaps conclude that such a church is behind the times. On the other hand, if they enter a church where women are openly and strongly involved in all facets of church life, a positive, subliminal message about that church will be exuded. "This church truly represents the whole Body of Christ."

Similar to the task of trying to attract singles and provide them with opportunities, church leaders must overcome certain biases or stereotypes in order to bring competent women into positions of leadership. They must anticipate opposition from more traditional-thinking members who may believe only men should lead and teach. Likewise, they must consciously dispel any stereotypical thinking and overgeneralization about women.

In addition to dealing with these negative attitudes towards women in church leadership positions, it is equally important for church leaders to create appropriate opportunities for women to be included in leadership. Similarly, churches should be creative in helping women to identify their spiritual gifts. Secondly, churches must be open to finding areas of service that may not be presently expressed in the congregation. In addition, churches should evaluate how well they're doing in addressing biases against women, and how consistently women are being considered for leadership and ministry roles.[21]

Similarly, William Easum claims that the traditional church women's groups don't meet the needs of baby boomer women. He believe's "today's women" need three things from the church: (1) practical "how-to" seminars in balancing career and home, parenting, values' clarification, support groups, and opportunities to come to terms with overcommitment; (2) powerful leadership roles that are challenging and give direction to the life of the church; and (3) schedules that take into accord her very busy life. The more institutional and denominational-based the material used by the women's groups, the less likely the groups will grow and attract baby boomer women.

Implications

The task facing churches who rush to attract the huge number of unchurched baby boomers will be extremely challenging. Only a minority of baby boomers have become loyal, committed worshipers. Another segment is still shopping around from one congregation to the next. And the largest segment of boomers is still exploring spiritual questions in its own highly individualistic way.[22]

Without a doubt, baby boomers will be the greatest potential source of church growth in the 90s. This generation is drastically different from any American generation alive today. Churches need to understand the unique futures of this generation and realize that baby boomers want goods and services styled for his or her needs and interests. A mass marketing or generic approach, while suitable in the past, will no longer work.

The churches that will prosper will be those that are "responsive" to the complex needs of baby boomers and attempt to more effectively satisfy these needs and wants. They will be responsive by understanding the unique characteristics of baby boomers, by trying to determine what their specific spiritual needs are, and by providing the types of worship, programs, spiritual opportunities, and relationships that baby boomers are seeking.

Likewise, such a church desiring to attract boomers must provide the type of environment that is comfortable, allows casual attire, yet places importance on building relationships. For those baby boomers who are searching for a church after having children, a church must recognize the necessity of a well-equipped, well-staffed daycare facility.

In addition, a huge opportunity awaits those churches who are sensitive and responsive to the needs of singles — one of the fastest growing segments of the population. Similarly, those searching for a church home may base their evaluation on the inclusion of women in ministry and leadership opportunities. If there is a lack of women involvement, it may signal the church as a male-dominated club and one of the greatest enemies of their personal liberty.

In essence, baby boomers, based on the sheer size of this generation and their diverse needs and wants, are shaping a new era for American religion. What has worked well for churches in the past may no longer be viable today. Unchurched baby boomers represent a golden opportunity to foster church growth. Whether churches can provide what it takes to attract boomers, keep them involved, and satisfy their spiritual and relational needs remains to be seen.

Endnotes

1. George Barna, "Seven Trends Facing the Church in 1988 and Beyond," *National & International Religion Report,* 1988, p. 3.

2. Richard N. Ostling, "The Generation That Forgot God," *Time,* April 5, 1993, p. 46.

3. Russell Chandler, *Racing Toward 2001,* Grand Rapids, MI: Zondervan Publishing House, p. 153.

4. Norman Shawchuck, Philip Kotler, Bruce Wrenn, Gustave Rath, *Marketing for Congregations.* Nashville TN: Abingdon Press, 1992, p. 65.

5. Wade Clark Roof, "The Baby Boomers' Search for God," *American Demographics,* December, 1992, p. 55.

6. Doug Morreau, *The Baby Boomers.* Ventura CA: Regal Books, 1990, p. 37.

7. *Ibid.,* p. 23.

8. Roof, *op. cit.,* p. 55.

9. Murreau, see p. 24.

10. Ostling, *op. cit,* p. 47.

11. William Easum, *How to Reach Baby Boomers.* Nashville TN: Abingdon Press, 1991, p. 109.

12. George Barna, *User Friendly Churches.* Ventura CA: Regal Books, 1991, p. 59.

13. Roof, see p. 54.

14. Ostling, *op. cit.,* p. 45.

15. Murren, *op. cit.,* p. 58.

16. George Barna, *Finding a Church You Can Call Home.* Ventura CA: Regal Books, 1992, p. 85.

17. Easum, *op. cit.,* p. 78

18. Easum, *op. cit.,* p. 32.

19. Easum, *op. cit.,* p. 85.

20. Murren, *op. cit.,* p. 38.

21. Murren, *op. cit.,* p. 181.

22. Roof, *op. cit.,* p. 57.

10

Benefits of a Marketing Orientation

Introduction

In the business sector, different companies became interested in marketing at different times. Marketing spread most rapidly in consumer purchased goods companies, consumer durables companies, and industrial equipment companies in that order. More recently, consumer service firms have moved toward modern marketing. The latest business groups to take an interest in marketing are professions such as lawyers, accountants, physicians, and architects. Finally, marketing is also attracting the interest of nonprofit organizations such as colleges, hospitals, police departments, museums, and symphonies.[1]

The above-mentioned examples illustrate how all types of businesses have willingly adopted a marketing orientation as a means to better identify the needs and wants of their intended publics and then systematically plan to develop the product/service that most effectively satisfies these needs. In today's competitive environment, firms can no longer ignore the actual needs and wants of the consumer, hoping that their product/service will be demanded by the public. The successful firms of tomorrow will be the ones that can successfully uncover gaps in the marketplace, or needs that have not been met or have been insufficiently met. Those products/services offered by the firms will be geared to satisfying such needs.

While churches certainly operate in a very unique environment compared to secular businesses, the lessons learned from other organizations regarding the benefits of a marketing orientation are extremely timely and essential for those churches seeking to make a difference in their communities.

The fact that the marketing concept has been broadened over the last several decades to include all types and sizes of organizations, both profit and nonprofit, infers that churches are no exception. What has worked well for other organizations in terms of their marketing strategy should and will work for those churches seeking to be more in touch with their constituents and desiring to provide the types of offerings that meet the spiritual and emotional needs of these individuals.

Throughout this book, a variety of marketing concepts, techniques, and strategies were discussed and their relevance to churches examined. The implications for churches following such an orientation were also offered. Those churches that decide to be more market-driven, while still remaining true Christ-serving churches, should experience numerous benefits as a result of this orientation. Just as the vast majority of other types of organizations have greatly benefited by adopting the marketing concept, so, too, should churches.

Specific Benefits

Those churches that become more marketing-oriented will very likely experience a great deal of change and should receive certain tangible and intangible benefits as a result of these decisions.

Clearer Vision

To begin with, a marketing-oriented church will likely develop a clearer vision for their ministry. The process of developing strategic plans for the church's offerings will undoubtedly provide a clear sense of direction or purpose. Planning implies the development of goals, objectives, strategies, and tactics, and provides a systematic process to move toward their intended purpose.

As stated previously, a church cannot be all things to all people. The benefits of a marketing-orientation will enable churches to best effectively allocate their available resources to provide the types of offerings or services that can help the church successfully work toward their intended mission. All churches operate under constraints of time, money, and staff. However, if a church knows where it's going and how it's going to get there, it will be much easier to conserve the available resources and use them more efficiently.

Sharper Focus

Many churches face declining membership in their congregations and will need to attract new individuals if they hope to survive in these turbulent times. Since most adults do not regularly attend church worship services, there appears to be a large untapped market for churches to pursue. However, in the secular world, today's successful markets are niche marketing. The concept of mass marketing, to treat everyone the same and appeal to all types of people, is no longer feasible. Churches wishing to grow and attract new members must understand these realities. Church leaders must understand the concept of market segmentation, the different ways to segment the market, and the different strategies to pursue the selected segments.

Just like their secular counterparts, churches must realize they can't be successful by treating the "unchurched" as one, single, undifferentiated mass in which everyone's spiritual and emotional needs are similar. The successfully growing churches of tomorrow will benefit by segmenting this large market in such a way that they can identify their appropriate target market and then determine what they must do to satisfy their particular needs and wants.

This sharper focus implied by segmenting the market and pursuing the desired target market(s) will enable the church to concentrate its efforts, prioritize, and have a much more significant impact on a smaller group of people. This infers that the church can achieve excellence in its ministry and make a focused effort in satisfying certain individuals' needs rather than spreading its limited resources too thin and accomplishing very little.

Effective Communication

The fact that a marketing-oriented church knows who it is trying to attract implies that such a sharper focus will enable it to more efficiently and effectively design the communication necessary to reach them. Rather than ineffectively trying to communicate to the masses about the church, its ministers, programs, and offerings, church leaders can pick the appropriate means of communication (or promotion) to most effectively reach the intended target market. Again, this implies a much more careful use of a church's limited resources and produces a much more significant impact.

Similarly, a marketing-oriented church will understand the value of clear and open communication to its current members. While trying to attract others, a church cannot ignore the congregation. Effective communication will keep members informed, involved, and feeling a vital part of the church community.

Increased Involvement

If a marketing-oriented church is successful in identifying the spiritual and emotional needs of its members and then able to provide the types of programs and services that address these needs, then such a church should enjoy increased involvement and participation from its members.

If members feel connected to other members and the church and enjoy a sense of community, it is obvious that they will be more willing to be involved in church-related activities and functions. Similarly, such members will also be more likely to volunteer for needed duties within the church, such as agreeing to teach Sunday School, act as greeters, help with the coffee hour, and serve on the various committees that are necessary in most churches, not to mention their increased willingness to support the church's ministry financially.

In addition, by addressing the actual needs of its members, a church should also sense a renewed enthusiasm among its constituents. A marketing-oriented church can fill a void in many members' lives and motivate and encourage them in their own "walk with God." Such renewed enthusiasm can also carry over in members' being more willing to reach out to others, both within the church and outside. If people feel good and enthusiastic about their church, they are more likely to communicate this joy to others. Unchurched friends may be curious about their friends' excitement about the church and the benefits they've obtained, and may just be intrigued enough to visit their friends' church to see what it's all about.

As stated previously, over 25% of unchurched Americans stated they would attend church if a close friend asked them. If such a friend is bursting with pride and enthusiasm about their church, then such an unchurched individual would likely be more willing to give it a try and take that initial step. Conversely, if the invited unchurched individual doesn't sense any joy or energy in their friend's description of the church, there would be little reason to change one's thinking about religion or ever consider how it might benefit them.

Positive Image in the Community

The numbers of unchurched Americans, while not belonging to or attending a particular church, still have perceptions of the churches in their community. Likely, they may perceive most churches to be very similar, merely representing different denominations, but not aware of any striking differences among the local churches.

An active, marketing-oriented church can stand out among other congregations and establish a somewhat unique, positive image in the eyes of the community. First, by satisfying the needs of its members, a church can become a symbol of a vital, healthy church. As mentioned previously, the enthusiasm, energy, and joy demonstrated by satisfied members is not only noticeable, but also somewhat contagious. The sharing of responsibilities, the willingness to participate, and the deepening commitment of its members will enable a church to provide even more programs and offerings that may benefit the entire community.

By reaching out to the local community and trying to help the myriad of problems present in the area, a local church can truly demonstrate "God's love." Such outreaches, done willingly and lovingly by the church's members will also be noticed by members of the community. Many unchurched individuals complain that the churches are always asking for money. How different will such an individuals' perception of a local church be when they witness the "random acts of kindness demonstrating God's love" that church members are providing without asking anything in return.

Such "servant evangelism" that is possible for a marketing-oriented church can represent a "differential advantage" when compared to other churches in the community. Those considering returning to church for whatever reason may be more inclined to visit such a church that is vital, healthy, concerned with the welfare of others, and appears to be made up of committed, caring individuals.

Numerical Growth

Stewart believes that while the market for churches hasn't changed, the market share has. As mentioned previously, many churches are plagued with declining membership leading to fewer resources that are needed to provide for a church's offerings. On the other hand, many of those churches that have achieved dramatic growth in membership tend to be marketing-oriented.

Such a phenomenon is logical when one considers that first, a marketing-oriented church is extremely involved in determining its members' needs and wants and then trying to satisfy these, subject to its own constraints. If the church is successful in providing the types of programs and offerings that meet its own members' needs and wants, then these individuals remain active, involved, and enthusiastic members. Similarly, as mentioned previously, the joy and enthusiasm may be evident to the members' friends and neighbors, possibly leading to their decision to visit the church.

Secondly, the marketing-oriented church, having segmented the market and knowing that segment of the community it hopes to attract, will be more focused on its efforts to attract newcomers. The active and vital image, the increased participation of the members, and the reaching out into the community by demonstrating "God's love," all benefits of a marketing-orientation, should help the church on its mission to attract newcomers and enlarge the "Kingdom of God."

In short, there are numerous tangible and intangible benefits resulting from a church becoming more marketing-oriented. However, there is nothing magical about marketing. A marketing orientation is not meant to replace the power of prayer, worship, vision, and one's commitment to God. Rather, it implies that church leaders use the resources provided as effectively and efficiently as possible. Church leaders can learn the techniques and strategies that have been successful for other profit and nonprofit firms and modify such knowledge to best accommodate their very unique environment without sacrificing their devotion and commitment to God.